The Macedonian national question in Greece in the documents of the Communist Party of Greece 1918–1940

The Macedonian national question in Greece in the documents of the Communist Party of Greece 1918–1940

Ireneusz Adam Ślupkov

Second enlarged edition

In memory of my great grandparents

Vasil and Vasilka Keramidžiev and

my beloved grandparents

Giorgi and Pena Ślupkov

Book reviewers

Prof. dr hab. Kole Simiczijew

Prof. dr Michael Seraphinoff
Prof. dr Zhidas Daskalovski

This book has been previously published under the title
"The Communist Party of Greece and the Macedonian national problem 1918–1940".
The second edition of this book has been changed and up-dated.

Ślupkov, Ireneusz Adam, 1965-
The Macedonian national question in Greece
in the documents of the Communist Party of Greece 1918–1940

ISBN: 978-0-359-32017-2

1. Macedonian-Communist movement.
2.Greece-Communist movement.
3.Macedonian-Ethnic Relations.
4. Greece-Ethnic relations.
5. Greece-Human Rights violation.

CONTENTS

INTRODUCTION

The subject of this book is the Communist Party of Greece (CPG) and the question of Macedonia between 1918 and 1940. The book is based on my master's thesis which was defended at the University of Szczecin in July 1993. However, the book differs significantly from the thesis. I have checked once again the translations of documents and made changes and additions where I have thought necessary. Fresh aspects of the problem were provided by Professor Kole Simiczijew, former lecturer in South Slavonic literatures at the University of Wrocław, Poland, who himself participated in the events described in this book. My thanks are also due to Professor Stojan Kiselinovski, my master and mentor, for friendship and many useful suggestions over all these years of acquaintanceship as well as to Professor Dragi Pop_Stefanija, Dana Lundmark, Slave Katin, Pavle Filipov-Voskopoulos and Risto Stefov for discussions about Macedonia. I should also like to express my deep gratitude to Mr G. T. Owen, the director of the British Council in Szczecin, Poland, in the years 1995-1998, who offered to translate the whole text into English and to Professor Michael Seraphinoff and Risto Stefov for checking my English translations to this enlarged edition of my book.

In this book I examine the way in which the CPG handled the Macedonian problem on the basis of documents released by the CPG, starting from the insurrection of 1918 and ending in 1940. These events are virtually unknown in English speaking countries. I have used publications mainly in Macedonian, Polish, Russian and English but my primary sources are the original documents of the CPG translated from Greek into Macedonian and then into English. Because these documents are unknown in the English speaking countries, my quotations from them have been translated into English. The translations may sometimes seem rather crude but this may probably be due to the uneven levels of education among members of the CPG. Moreover, the documents have been translated from Greek into Macedonian and then into English.

The documents show the influence of the Comintern on the CPG as well as internal conflict between the two factions, the so-called "*majority*" and "*minority*", as well as their policies towards the Macedonian question.

These materials have been selected and translated by the Macedonian historian Professor Risto Kirjazovski of the National Historical Institute in Skopje in Macedonia under the title "*KPG i makedonskoto nacionalno prašanje 1919-1974*" Skopje 1982.

Another important source is that of the Macedonian historian and authority on the history of the CPG's handling of the Macedonian problem, Professor Stojan Kiselinovski; "*Egejskiot del na Makedonija (1913-1989)*", "*Etničkite promeni vo Makedonija (1913-1995)*".

A more thorough investigation of how the CPG treated the Macedonian problem has now been made possible by the

Macedonian government's purchase in the beginning of the 70s of all the original documents of the CPG.

This book consists of an introduction, five chapters conclusion and maps of the territory under discussion. The first chapter deals with the problem of nationalities in Europe immediately after the first world war and the policies of the Comintern. This chapter is necessary for an understanding of what follows. The second chapter deals with the handling of the Macedonian problem by the CPG between 1918 and 1924. The third chapter covers the period 1924 to 1931/5 which was marked by changes in the CPG's approach to the Macedonian problem. The fourth chapter examines the events of the years 1931-40 in which an ideological "breakthrough" occurred. Some attention is also paid to the formation of the Macedonian Patriotic Party (VMRO) in Aegean (Greek) Macedonia and its activities amongst Macedonians. In the fifth chapter the real motives for the CPG's change of support from the slogan "United and Independent Macedonia" to "Equal Rights for Minorities" are explained.

The history of the CPG's relations with Macedonian question in Greece are best followed chronologically. Some of the documents bear only initials or surnames so authorship cannot always be identified. Names are given in the original or in transliteration. Greek place names, obligatory since 1917, are given next to Macedonian names. The accompanying maps show their locality. In the translations of the documents, the original style and phraseology has been retained as far as possible. Macedonian letters should be pronounced as follows; dž – dj, ž - zh, č - ch, š - sh.

Greek 'dh' and 'gh' are velarised versions of 'd' and 'g'.

The author's comments and additions are in square brackets.

CHAPTER

1

THE PROBLEM OF NATIONALITIES IN EUROPE AND THE POLICY OF THE COMINTERN

At the end of the first world war, Europe was faced with a difficult task, that of creating a new world order to take account of political and geographical changes in Europe. There was also the question of creating new nations with partly homogeneous nationalities. It was hoped that these problems would be solved at the Versailles peace conference which would provide a cure for all the festering wounds of Europe at the time.[1] In the event the Peace Conference[2] in which 32 countries[3] participated solved nothing and the question of nationalities dragged on until the outbreak of the second world war. The source of these conflicts were the following territorial conflict between ;

- France and Germany over Alsace-Lorraine,
- Hungary and Romania over Transylvania,
- Hungary and Czechoslovakia over Ukrainian Transcarpathia,
- Yugoslavia and Hungary over Voivodina,
- Yugoslavia and Austria over Carinthia,

---

1 J Pajewski, Historia powszechna 1871–1918, Warszawa 1967, p. 453.

2 en.wikipedia.org/wiki/Paris_Peace_Conference,_1919
http://en.wikipedia.org/wiki/Treaty_of_Versailles
On conference in the Greek aspect see. M. L. Smith, The Ionian vision. Greece in Asia minor 1919-1922, C. Hurst & Co., London 2005, pp. 62–85 also M. MacMillan, Paris 1919, Random House, New York 2002, pp. 347–365.

3 J. S. Schapiro, Modern and contemporary European history (1815–1928), The Riberside Press, Cambridge, Massachusetts, 1929, p. 741.

- Albania and Yugoslavia over Kosovo,
- Yugoslavia and Italy over Istria,
- Italy and Austria over South Tyrol,
- between Bulgaria and Greece over Western Thrace,
- between the Soviet Union and Romania over Bessarabia and Northern Bukovina,
- between Poland and the Soviet Union over the Curzon Line
- between Poland and Germany over Upper Silesia and Pomerania.

In addition there were five major nationality disputes to be settled; the Macedonians, the Basques[4] the Catalans[5], the Flemings[6] and the Jews[7] and two minor; the Lemko[8] (Ruthenian) and the Sorbian[9] (Wendish). All these problems, including the latter, were essentially of both a territorial and a national nature. Thus it was that the recipe for permanent political instability was written into the history of Europe from the very start of the new post-war epoch.[10] In Southern Europe there was not one state which was able to claim a majority of any nationality.

---

4 Basques C. Watson, Modern Basque history: eighteenth century to the present, University of Nevada Press 2003 M. Kurlansky, The Basque history of the world, Walker & Company, New York 1999.

5 J. Stefanowicz, Bunt mniejszości. Współczesne separatyzmy narodowe.Warszawa 1977, pp. 363–367.

6 Ibidem, pp. 166 –168, S Kiselinovski, KPG i makedonskoto nacionalno prašanje 1918–1940, Skopje 1985, p. 27.

7 S. Sierpowski, Między wojnami 1919–1939, Część 1: lata 1919–1929, Wyd. Kurpisz, Poznań 1998, pp. 54–62.

8 B. Horbal, Sprawa łemkowska na konferencji pokojowej w Paryżu w 1919 roku, Wrocławskie Studia Wschodnie 8 (2004), WUW 2004, pp. 139–163.

9 G. Wyder, Kwestia łużycka w świetle literatury historycznej okresu miedzywojennego (próba wstępnej analizy), Wyższa Szkoła Pedagogiczna im. T. Kotarbińskiego, Zielona Gora 1998, D. Matelski, Tożsamość narodowa i procesy integracyjne Serbołużyczan w Rzeszy Niemieckiej (od średniowiecza do współczesności), p. 109.

10 ibid.

Central Europe

The countries of Central Europe were better off; the percentage of the native population of Finland comprised 89.3%, of Estonia 88.2%, of Bulgaria 83.2%, of Latvia 80.4%, of Romania 76%, of Poland 69.1% but of Czechoslovakia and Yugoslavia only 42%.[11] With such figures, it would not have been difficult to predict conflict which in fact arose almost as soon as these states were established.[12]

Balkans

The Balkans provided a good example of the unresolved problems of nationality and territory. One of the worst consequences of the Versailles conference was that it failed to establish any Balkan state with a homogeneous population. Only "*natural*" states enjoyed some semblance of stability. Yugoslavia for example in 1924 had a population of 12,055,688 but no nation within Yugoslavia comprised more than 50% of the population. Some 7 million people, Croatians, Macedonians, Slovenians, Montenegrins and Albanians had a sense of separate identity.[13] A similar situation obtained in Romania. So-called "Greater Romania" absorbed South Dobrudža Transylvania, Bessarabia, South Bukovina and the

---

[11] ibid. pp. 7–8.

[12] H Batowski, Rozpad Austro-Węgier 1914–1918, Kraków 1982, p. 291.

[13] S Kiselinovski, os. cit., p. 28.

Romanian parts of the Banat and thus became a multinational country.

In the Kingdom of Romania there lived one and a half million Hungarians, 800,000 Germans, 400,000 Bulgarians, 300,000 Ruthenians and more than a million Jews scattered throughout the whole territory of the kingdom.[14]

The Kingdom of Greece

The Kingdom of Greece also moved into territory which had never had any Greek ethnicity[15] and thus, as in the case of Romania, no homogeneous Greek character.

Map.1 The Greek territorial gains 1821–1917

Source: :http://commons.wikimedia.org/wiki/File:Greekhistory.GIF [download: 30.11.2011].

Greece only possessed a homogeneous Greek population in the territory of what was Ancient Greece, namely the Peloponese, Southern Epirus and

[14] ibid.

[15] ibid.

Thessaly as far as Olympus. Everything north of these territories had no Greek identity. Thus Northern Epirus, for example, was inhabited by Albanians and Macedonia by Macedonians[16], often called Slavo-Macedonians while Thrace was inhabited by Turks and Bulgarians. According to the Bulgarian scholar Vasil Kynčov, the population of Aegean (Greek) Macedonia in 1913 consisted of 358,290 Bulgarians, (49.92%), 218,747 Greeks (30.48%), 59,720 Jews (8.32%), 34,427 Vlachs (4.8%), 30,726 Gypsies (4.29%), 6,875 Albanians (0.95%) and 8,910 other nationalities comprising 1.24% of the general population. (See graph below)

Graph 1.Ethnic composition of Aegean (Greek) Macedonia in 1913

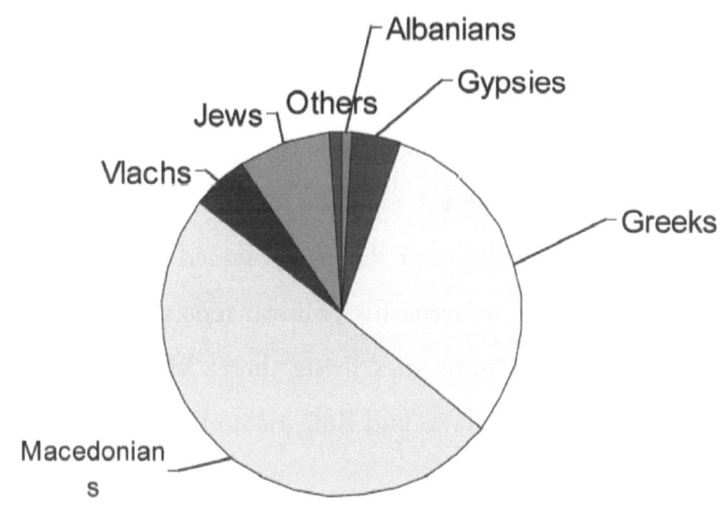

Source: S. Kiselinovski, Egejskiot del na Makedonija(1918-1989), Skopje 1990, p. 9.

[16] Narody mira istoriko–etnografičeskij spravočnik, Moskva 1988, pp. 272-273, Ludy i języki swiata, Warszawa 2000, p. 133.

As his criterion for ethnicity, Kynčov disregarded the language spoken at school[17] (Greek, Serbian or Bulgarian) and religious affiliation and used the language spoken at home. The Greek authorities however used the language spoken at school as their criterion for ethnicity. Hence the divergence between Greek and Bulgarian statistics.[18] Moreover, Bulgarian scholars have made and continue to make the error of regarding Macedonian as a dialect of Bulgarian. As a result, Macedonians living in Aegean (Greek) Macedonia are considered to be indigenous Bulgarians. Thus about a million people of non-Greek origin lived in Aegean Macedonia and Western Thrace during the 1920.[19]

Bulgaria

As far as Bulgaria is concerned, here too the population was not homogeneous. Turks, Macedonians and Armenians formed 16.8% of people living in Bulgaria. Such were the results of the treaty signed at Neuilly-sur-Seine.[20] The Balkans thus became an arena for political repression or, at the very least, political exploitation of minorities living there. Macedonians fell victims to repression in Greece, Yugoslavia and Bulgaria and Croats, Slovenes,

[17] S Kiselinovski, Egejskiot del na Makedonija (1913–1989), Skopje 1990, p. 9.

[18] On differences in statistics see I. Stawowy-Kawka, *Macedonia w polityce państw bałkańskich w XX wieku,* Kraków 1993, pp. 17–20, *Ludność Macedonii–zmiany struktury narodowościwej w XX wieku,* in Dzieje Najnowsze 2-1998, Warszawa 1998, *Historia Macedonii,* Ossolineum, Wrocław 2000, p. 131, T. Wituch, *Tureckie przemiany. Dzieje Turcji 1878–1923,* Warszawa 1980, p. 92, A. Giza, *Stosunki narodowościowe na ziemiach macedońskich na początku XX wieku,* Balcanica Posnaniensia XI/XII, UAM, Poznań 2001, pp.129–135, T. Kostopoulos, *Counting the „Other": Official Census and Classified Statistics in Greece (1830–2001)* in „JGKS" no 5/2003 pp.55–78.

[19] S Kiselinovski, KPG i makedonskoto... p. 28.

[20] ibid. p. 29.

Montenegrins and Albanians in Yugoslavia as well as Hungarians in Romania. The result was that they began to dream of creating their own independent countries.[21]

These unresolved questions attracted the attentions of those countries which had lost the war as well as the Communist International (the Comintern). The former made use of the peace treaties to revise international frontiers while the latter, under Lenin's guidance, saw opportunities to spread propaganda on the theme of national self-determination which, by appearing to offer one solution to the manifold problems caused by injustice, exploitation and pauperisation, served to attract thousands of people to the Communist Party in the Balkans.[22]

Europe

Let us return to the general political situation obtaining at the time in Europe. The group of vanquished nations expressed dissatisfaction with the resolutions of the peace treaties signed in Paris. These nations included Germany, Bulgaria and Hungary. In 1919 they began to agitate for changes to the treaties (signed at Versailles, Trianon, Neuilly and St Germain)[23] because they considered them to be detrimental to their interests.

---

21 Vasil Kolarov, Natsionalny Vopros na Balkanach, Kommunističny Internatsional 1924, Nr. 3-4 in Kiselinovski, KPG i makedonskoto…, p. 29.

22 W I Lenin, O prawie narodów do samookreślenia, Warszawa 1952.

23 S Kiselinovski, KPG i makedonskoto...,p. 29.

Germany laid claim to Alsace and Lorraine in France, to Eupen and Malmedy in Belgium, to Gdańsk and Upper Silesia in Poland and to the Sudeten in Czechoslovakia. The Kingdom of Bulgaria also raised objections to the frontiers defined at Neuilly and laid claim to South Dobrudža which had been allocated to Romania as well as to Vardar Macedonia which had been given to the Kingdom of the Serbs, Croats and Slovenes (from 1929, Yugoslavia) and to Aegean (Greek) Macedonia and Western Thrace which formed part of Greece. Hungary also laid claim to territory ceded in the treaty of Trianon.[24] This included up to 75% of its historical lands; Transylvania (ceded to Romania) and Voivodina (part of Yugoslavia). It also claimed territory in Southern Slovakia.[25]

Map 2. Territories lost by Hungary

Source: http://commons.wikimedia.org/wiki/File:Dissolution_of_Austria-Hungary.png [download: 30.11.2011]

---

[24] On the Hungarian position during the talks in Trianon see Ignac Romsics, Hungary in the Twentieth century, Corvina/Osiris, Budapest, 1999, pp. 117–125

[25] ibid.

All these plans to revise the frontiers did not meet with the approval of other states. On the contrary, France, Britain, Yugoslavia, Greece, Romania and Czechoslovakia opposed any revisions of the boundaries agreed at Versailles. The period between the wars was thus marked by bitter clashes between those countries urging boundary revisions and those countries defending the status quo laid down at Versailles. The situation gave rise to serious political friction and, as a result, political instability[26] which was quite contrary to the aim of the Versailles treaty which was to create a new order for Europe. A new and totally unforeseen factor in this new order was the Soviet Union whose distinct ideology introduced more problems and complications into European politics than anybody could have predicted.

In view of the Soviet Union's distinct ideological stance, it could not nor did not guarantee the resolutions of the Versailles treaty and furthermore expressed its dissatisfaction with the distribution of territories in Europe because it ignored the principle, upheld by Lenin, of the right of national self-determination. The USSR also laid claims to the territories of its neighbours, those for example of Poland (the question of Vilnius, Western Belarus and Western Ukraine), Romania (Bessarabia, Northern Bukovina) and Czechoslovakia (Transcarpathian Ukraine). Nor was the USSR willing to tolerate its isolation, both political and economic, which had been brought about with a view to causing its collapse.[27] As it happened, the USSR

---

[26] ibid. p. 30.

[27] ibid.

overcame this problem by reaching an agreement with Germany in Rappallo in 1922.[28]

Stalin maintained that to build socialism and at the same time weaken the western powers, the USSR had to adopt policies which would foment unrest among the signatory countries of the Versailles treaty leading to political destabilisation and increased national and class struggle. These policies, he maintained, would weaken those countries' aggressive stance towards the USSR.[29] An excellent means of attaining this end was the creation of the Comintern[30] and the Balkan Communist Federation (BCF).[31] The aim of the Comintern was to promote Lenin's policy of world revolution whereas the aim of the BCF was to turn the whole of the Balkans into a soviet republic. As a result of these aims being adopted both by the Comintern and the BCF, Stalin's aims were fully realised. Under their auspices, the USSR planned to subvert the whole world, thereby creating communist regimes dependent on the USSR. The BCF's task was to bring about a communist revolution in the Balkans and create a Balkan Soviet Socialist Republic. The BCF upheld the demands of all peoples living in the Balkans for self-determination, particularly those of the Macedonians,[32] a people spread over four states, Albania, Bulgaria, Greece and Yugoslavia. As mentioned earlier,[33] the neglect of these problems

---

28 H Batowski, Między dwiema wojnami, 1919-1939, Kraków, 1988, pp. 107–109.

29 S Kiselinovski, ibid.

30 World Communism. A Handbook 1918-1965, ed. W S Sworakowski, Hoover Institutions Press, Stanford 1973, pp. 78–91.

31 ibid. pp. 29–30.

32 ibid.

33 See below chapter 4.

of nationality provided the Comintern with excellent opportunities of putting their programmes into action with an almost 100 percent chance of success.

The years 1935 to 1939 brought political changes as a result of the growing influence of fascist regimes. The Comintern's efforts were devoted to a struggle with these regimes leading to changes of policy and abandonment of previously held positions, especially those relating to self-determination for minor nationalities.[34] Before that however, the unresolved nationality problems of such peoples as the Macedonians, Croatians, Ukrainians, Belarussians, Slovenes, Albanians, Bulgarians and Hungarians brought about destabilisation in post-Versailles Europe. The gravity of these problems was underlined by the Fifth Congress of the Comintern, held in Moscow in 1924, which was entirely devoted to this theme. Particular attention was paid to the questions of Hungarians in Romania, Czechoslovakia and Yugoslavia, Ukrainians and Belarussians in Poland, Bulgarians in Thrace and South Dobrudža, Macedonians in Greece, Bulgaria and the Kingdom of Serbs, Croats and Slovenes, and Croats, Montenegrins and Albanians in Yugoslavia. Dmitriy Manuilskiy emphasised that "*the revolt of the peoples is a bomb we can plant with the aim of causing revolution in Europe*". The Comintern further decided that instead of the social and national discrimination prevailing in Europe after 1919, it would follow, together with the BCF, the path of socialist revolution fighting for liberty and equal rights for all peoples of the Balkan-Danube area and their right to self-determination.[35] Moreover they demanded the right of all people in this area to be united in a Balkan-

[34] P Poulipoulos, Ghia to Makedhoniko, Artha, Thesis kai Polemikes, Athina 1976, p. 76.

[35] Kommunističeski Internatsional, 1920, No. 14 in S Kiselinovski, ibid, p. 32.

Danubian Soviet Socialist Republic.[36] The oppressed peoples living in Greece, Yugoslavia, Romania, Czechoslovakia and Poland would be granted the right to self-determination.[37] As far as Croats, Montenegrins and Slovaks were concerned, the Comintern not only recognised their rights to self-determination but also their rights to establish their own states in the countries in which they were already living. At the same time, the right of Hungarians living in Romania, Czechoslovakia and the Kingdom of the Serbs, Croats and Slovenes to self-determination and union with Hungary was recognised. However the question of Macedonia was raised for the first time and very carefully considered at the Fifth Congress. It was noted that their dispersal was the very factor which strengthened their desire for a united homeland divided between Albania, Yugoslavia, Greece and Bulgaria. The Fifth Congress therefore confirmed the right to self-determination and the simultaneous creation of an independent Macedonian state as well as a Balkan Federation of equal and independent worker and peasant republics.[38] The BCF adopted the resolutions which were passed at the Fifth Comintern Congress at its own Sixth Congress and declared that the "*policy of the communist parties regarding the desire of the Macedonians for their own united and independent state is just and fair*".[39] The adoption by the BCF of the resolutions concerning

---

36 ibid.

37 5-ti Vsyemirny Kongryes Kommunističeskogo Internatsionala, Tezisy, Ryezolutsii i Postanovleniya, Moskva 1924 in Kiselinovski ibid.

38 Ch. Balkanskaya Kommunističeskaya Federatsiya, Gozisdat RSFSR, Moskwa 1930 in D G Kousoulas, Revolution and Defeat, OUP, London 1965, p. 60.

39 The Communist International, 1924, No. 7, p. 95. in S Kiselinovski ibid p. 32.

Macedonia was not unanimous and objections were raised.[40] Such resistance had been expected given the interests of other states and nationalities, especially in the Balkans, as well as certain Party members,[41] but there was also no agreement to accept these resolutions as binding. The Bulgarian Communist Party was keenly interested in the Macedonian question given the fact that after the Treaties of Versailles and Neuilly, Bulgaria had lost much of its territory to its neighbours. Romania had been given Dobrudža, Greece Aegean (Greek) Macedonia and Thrace and the Kingdom of Serbs, Croats and Slovenes Vardar Macedonia to which Bulgaria had laid claim as well.[42] Bulgaria was also dissatisfied with this solution of the Macedonian question because Macedonians were considered to be Bulgarians. There was of course a degree of political manoeuvring in this context because in reality the Bulgarians considered the Macedonians to be a distinct if slightly retarded ethnic element compared with true Bulgarians. But officially, Macedonia was considered to be Bulgarian territory. It is thus understandable that the Bulgarian Communist Party (CPB) could not afford not to take a position on this important and sensitive issue and thus declared that all the above-mentioned territory was ethnically and historically Bulgarian. Taking its cue from the Comintern, the CPB demanded the creation of a united and independent Macedonia and similarly for Thrace and Dobrudža. It was therefore plainly demonstrated that the CPB was bravely defending national interests.

---

40 S Kiselinovski, KPG i makedonskoto..., p. 30.

41 See below chapter three

42 T Wasilewski, Historia Bułgarii, Wrocław 1988, p. 240.

Map 3. Lands lost by Bulgaria

Source: http://commons.wikimedia.org/wiki/File:Bulgaria_after_Treaty_of_Neuilly-sur-Seine.png [download: 30.11.2011].

In pursuing the policy of the establishment of new states, Bulgaria was seeking its own advantage. Let us examine this more closely. If a united and independent Macedonia were to be established, then this would automatically weaken the Kingdom of Serbs, Croats and Slovenes.[43] If a united and independent Thrace were to be created, then this would be to the detriment of Greece and Turkey. In both cases, Bulgaria would emerge in a strengthened position. At the same time the CPB would support the territorial claims of Hungary to Romania concerning Transylvania and to Yugoslavia concerning Voivodina as well as those of the USSR to Romania concerning Bessarabia. All

43 S Kiselinovski os. cit p. 33.

this was calculated to weaken Bulgaria's natural enemies, namely the Kingdom of Serbs, Croats and Slovenes, Greece and Romania and strengthen her natural allies, namely Hungary and the USSR.[44]

As far as a united and independent Macedonia was concerned, the BCP considered the territory to be "*populated by Bulgarians*". Obviously such a view provoked opposition from the Communist Parties of Greece and Yugoslavia (CPG and CPY). In this situation the Comintern attempted to reconcile the divergent views of the Balkan parties with regard to the Macedonian question. Unrelenting pressure by the Comintern on these parties achieved results. During the Fifth Congress of the Balkan Communist Federation in 1922, a consensus was reached about the formation of a united and independent Macedonia. This consensus however was fatally compromised. It emerged that all nationalities living in the Balkans would co-exist in Macedonia and no one nationality would have an absolute majority. The result was that whichever nationality would predominate in Macedonia, (Serbs, Bulgarians or Greeks), the others would automatically be discriminated against. The Sixth Congress of the CBF therefore declared that the establishment of a single, united and independent Macedonia under the auspices of the Balkan Federation would ensure the rights and liberties of all nationalities.[45] Thanks to this solution, the BCF accepted the statement that different nationalities lived in Macedonia. However, the Communist Parties of Greece and Yugoslavia accepted the policy of a united and independent Macedonia which in the framework of the Balkan Federation would have to guarantee peaceful development of all

---

[44] ibid.

[45] Žurnal Kommunističeski Internatsional, 1924, No. 3-4 in ibid. p. 34.

peoples living in Macedonia. Despite this compromise, voices of protest began to be raised immediately after the Sixth Congress. These protests came from different nationalities and different countries in the Balkans but the most vociferous opposition to the concept of a united and independent Macedonia came from the ranks of the Communist Party of Greece.[46]

[46] ibid. p. 35.

CHAPTER

2

THE COMMUNIST PARTY OF GREECE (CPG) AND ITS POLICY OF "NEITHER STATEHOOD NOR NATIONHOOD" (1918–24)

In order to comprehend the position of the CPG with regard to Macedonia, it is necessary to recall the main political themes in Greece before and after the uprising of 1830. The concept of the so-called "*Great Idea*" (meaning a Greater Greece) was present in Greek political thought throughout the 19th and early 20th centuries. It was also accepted by the CPG even though its origins were to be found in Greek bourgeois circles and thus inimical to the Communists. The concept itself (Gr Meghali Idhea Μεγάλη Ιδέα) came from the Phanariots, members of the old Byzantine aristocracy living in Constantinople (Tur Istanbul) who took their name from the area of the city, Phanar, in which they lived. Here too was, and still is, the seat of the Greek Patriarchy which administered to the orthodox churches of the Middle East. The Phanariots[47] were closely linked to the Patriarchy and supported it financially, thus enabling them to wield influence over the whole Greek

[47] See The New Encyclopedia Britannica, Micropaedia Vol. III, 1975, p. 925.

orthodox church. Not all this interest was beneficial to the church.[48] Aided and abetted by the orthodox church, they wished to assert its supremacy over the non-Greek church by forbidding, among other measures, the use of vernacular languages in the liturgy and insisting on the use of Greek [called katharevousa (*pure Greek*) which was used only by an intellectual elite and was not understood by ordinary people who used Greek called dhimotiki (*popular Greek*)]. Gradually, the Phanariots became civil servants in the imperial Ottoman administration. From 1699 to 1821 they held the offices of Dragomans and Hospodars.[49] Dragomans were both interpreters, political advisors and secretaries of state. Hospodars were directly responsible to the Ottoman authorities and ruled the principalities of Walachia and Moldavia in their names. Their superior education and knowledge both of Balkan and western European languages and western thought enabled them to wield considerable power even though they were in theory captive subjects of the Turks. It was no accident, therefore, that plans for the rebirth of Greece were first mooted among their ranks. They founded secret societies, so-called "*heteries*" whose task it was to prepare Greeks, step by step, for a national uprising. This task only became possible during the 19th century when the Ottoman Empire had begun to decline.

---

48 L.S. Stavrianos, *The Balkans since 1953*, p. 271, *By the end of the seventeenth century these laymen filled all the important administrative offices of the church, which meant that they managed church properties and revenues, supervised the monasteries, safeguarded the valuable liturgical objects, and so forth. Having gained control of the church administration, the Phanariote laymenthen proceeded to intervene in the election of bishops, archbishops, and even patriarchs. By exerting pressure upon the Church Synod, which elected the Patriarch of Constantinople, they were able to influence decisively the selection of the head of the church. They were able to do this easily and effectively because of their commanding position within the church and their wealth and influence without.* See further in "Enghromi Enkiklopedia Idhroghios, tomos 15, Ekdhosis <Dhomiki>, Athina 1982, p. 160.

49 See J Demel, Historia Rumunii, Wrocław 1986, pp. 215–216.

The best example of their increasing influence was the creation of the "*Republic of the United Seven Islands*" (the Ionian Islands)[50] under the terms of the Russo-Turkish treaty of 21 March 1800. This was to be a first step in the gradual process of winning back territory under Turkish rule. The Phanariots, who initiated this process, together with the church hierarchy, adumbrated the so-called "*Great Idea*" (Greater Greece). In historical perspective, the idea may be a fantasy but it nevertheless found many supporters, particularly among adherents of the future Greek monarchy, including King Otto and his successor George I.[51] The "*Great Idea*" envisaged the extension of the Kingdom of Greece to the Adriatic Sea in the west, to the Black Sea in the east and to the Mediterranean Sea in the south. In other words, they took as a territorial basis for a reconstituted Greece the Byzantine Empire at its fullest extent. In so doing, they ignored the fact that these territories were only under Byzantine rule for a limited period and, moreover, were ethnically never Greek[52] . In such areas as Northern Epirus, Macedonia, Thrace and Anatolia (now in Turkey), Greeks lived only on the peripheries. They never lived in the core of these territories. None of this however presented a problem for the proponents of the "*Great Idea*". The Macedonians, like other nations, were characterised according to this theory as "*slavophones*" (Greek slavophon

---

50 H Batowski, Państwa bałkańskie 1800–1923, Kraków 1938, pp. 9–10.

51 ibid. pp 91–92. See also Enghromi Enkiklopedia Idhroghios, tomos 10, Ekdhosis <Dhomiki> Athina 1982, p. 143.

52 „Except for the islands and the southern part of the peninsula, where the population was mainly Greek, and for the regions north of the Aimos mountains, where the Slav element was dominant, the great bulk of the Balkans was inhabited by a heterogeneous mixture of Greeks, Serbs, Bulgarians, Wallachians, Rumanians, Albanians and of course Turks – the Greek element being more concentrated in the towns and along the coasts, and the Slavs becoming more numerous in the mountains and plains of the interior. Greek predominance was greatest in Constantinople and the few large commercial and cultural centres of the Ottoman Empire: Salonica, Ioannina, Adrianople, Philippoupolis, Iassi, Smyrna, Alexandria".

meaning Slavic-speaker) or as "*foreign language speakers*" (Greek alophon meaning alien, foreign speaker). They all had to be hellenised[53] and this was done by establishing various educational institutions and above all by setting up Greek schools and consulates in non-Greek territories with a view to realising the "*Great Idea*". After 1870, Greek activities to achieve this aim gradually began to increase. Despite Greek efforts, the Macedonians retained their feeling of separateness as the Macedonian insurrection of 2 August 1903[54] abundantly demonstrated. It broke out on St Elijah's day (Mac. Ilindenskoto vostanie) and is thus known as the Elijah Uprising.

Nikola Karev

Goce Delčev

Source:
https://mk.wikipedia.org/w/index.php?title=Податотека:Nikola_Karev.jpg&filetimestamp=20100729130723 [download: 30.11.2011].
https://mk.wikipedia.org/w/index.php?title=Податотека:G_Delchev.jpg&filetimestamp=20080114044323 [downloaded: 30.11.2011].

---

[53] See R Poplazarov, Grčka politika sprema Makedonija vo vtorata polovina na XIX i početokot na XX vek. This book gives a good description of the influence of the "Great Idea" on Greek political life. It accurately demonstrates Greek expansionism in Macedonia.

[54] J Skowronek, M Tanty, T Wasilewski, Historia Słowian południowych i zachodnich, Warszawa 1988, p. 510.

The Macedonians wished to demonstrate to the whole of Europe that they wanted a separate and independent state that would not be part of Albania, Greece, Serbia or Bulgaria. Although the uprising failed after three months, the fact that it had occurred strengthened the Macedonian's demands for independence. Greece realised that it would have to restrict its policies to opening schools on Macedonian territory rather than forcing a wholesale hellenisation of the Macedonian people. They thus organised military units of Greek "*andarts*", and started the so called the Greek struggle (Gr. Μακεδονικός Αγώνας)[55] for Macedonia (1904-1908). Andarts were Greek officers for the most part who were sent to Macedonia to terrorise and kill the innocent civilian population (the most famous slaughter took place at the place of Zagoričani)[56] and force them to abandon their national aspirations and become Greek "*on return to Greece*".[57]

Especially two persons were responsible for terror and killings of the civilian population. First was the Metropolitan Ghermanos Karavanghelis[58] from the town of Kostur (Kastoria) who organized and coordinated the struggle in Greek Macedonia. He became famous for his enormous cruelty, which, among other things he paid for cutting the heads of Macedonian fighters who fought for an independent Macedonia, heads that were brought to him to be exposed to others. About all these cruelties towards Macedonians,

---

[55] H. Batowski, Państwa bałkańskie 1800–1923, Kraków 1938, pp. 9–10.

[56] See D. Lithoxou, Ellinikos antimakedhonikos aghonas A'. Apo to 'Ilinten sti Zagkoritsani (1903–1905).

[57] See S. Kiselinovski, Egejskot del na Makedonija 1918–1989, Skopje 1990 pp. 19–42.

[58] See D. Ljorovski-Vamvakovski, Germanos Karavangelis. Grčkata propaganda vo Kosturska eparhija (1900—1903).

whom he called Bulgarians, he wrote in his memoirs, information later used and cited by author Gheorgios Nakratzas.[59] Nakratzas dealing with the ethnic as well as the original problems or losing its own language (language shift) by influence of the different nations living in the Balkans and being forced to accept different languages and as a consequence of changing its own national identity. It is probably the first book published in Greece which questions a great deal of myths regarding the modern Greeks "*racial purity*" as well as those in the various other Balkan nations.

The second person was a Greek officer named Pavlos Melas[60] who was one of the first officers to organize an armed unit to fighting against the Macedonian Komitadzhis, komitadzi[61] or komits[62]. He was killed by the Turks

---

59 G. Nakratzas, The close racial kinship…, p. 90. The barbarity with which each faction dealt with its rivals was unprecedented. The exploits of the Greek side at least are described by the Metropolitan of Kastoria, Yermanos Karavangelis himself, in his memoirs, in a manner that is more appropriate to the Dark Ages than to a man of God. He cynically describes how he wrecked the Bulgarian high school in Kastoria with his own hands, and follows this with: „*Then we killed the director general of the Bulgarian Committee for Kastoria and Florina, Lazo Trajkov…they cut off his head and brought it to the Cathedral.* W: G. Karavanghelis, Apomnimonevmata, O Makedhonikos aghonas, sel. 52. However Evangelos Kofos in his book *Nationalism and Communism in Macedonia. Civil conflict, politics of mutation, national identity*, Aristide D. Caratzas, New York 1993 states on page 34 that *The most capable of them all was Germanos Karavangelis, who was appointed bishop of Kastoria in 1900[59], at the age of 34.* One of his first successful undertakings was the formation of Slavophone Greek bands to protect the villages of his diocese against the comitadjis. The book is full of distortions, extreme opinions and racially biased information. The Macedonians were treated as Bulgarians. Unfortunately this book, for many years, was the only source of information available to West European and American universities which dealt with the Macedonian question in Greece. Evangelos Kofos was responsible for the creation of Greek policy towards the Macedonian question. He was and is still regarded as a "*specialist*" in the Macedonian question.

60 http://en.wikipedia.org/wiki/Pavlos_Melas

61 http://en.wikipedia.org/wiki/Komitadji

62 http://sr.wikipedia.org/sr/Komiti

in the village Statitsa (Melas) located in Kostur Region[63]. In Greece both these men are regarded as national heroes.

Ghermanos Karavanghelis

Source: http://en.wikipedia.org/wiki/File:Germanos_Karavaggelis2.jpg [download: 30.11.2011].

Post card with photo Pavlos Melas

Source: http://en.wikipedia.org/wiki/File:Pavlos_melas.jpg[download date: 30.11.2011].

63 http://en.wikipedia.org/wiki/Kastoria

This was what the "*Great Idea*" meant in practice on territory which had never been Greek. After the Balkan wars of 1912/13, however, some success in this direction was achieved. Two factors were instrumental. The first was the movement of Greek-speaking Greeks and Turks or Christian population;

Armenians, Lazi[64], Cappadocian Greeks living in Cappadocia[65]- speaking Byzantine Greek[66] with big mixture of Turkish in grammar as well as phonetics, Ponti (Pondi) Greeks originating from the ancient city of Pont by the Black Sea speaking older form of Greek [mixture of Attic, Koine, Byzantine Greek, Turkish, Persian and Caucasian languages] not understood by mainland Greeks, Turkish-speaking Greeks, Turks, and Orthodox ethnically mixed population from the province of Karaman called Karamanli[67] [mixture of Greeks, Turks and Persians] using in speech Turkish language but writing with the help of the Greek alphabet and called in Greek "*prosphighi*" using in speech Turkish language but writing with the help of the Greek alphabet and in Macedonian "*madžiri*" (refugees) from Turkey to Aegean(Greek) Macedonia.[68] In the years 1913–1928 618.199 of Christian population was displaced altogether in Aegean Macedonia.[69]

---

[64] http://en.wikipedia.org/wiki/Laz_people

[65] http://en.wikipedia.org/wiki/Cappadocia

[66] http://en.wikipedia.org/wiki/Cappadocian_Greek_language

[67] A. N. Karakasidou, Fields of wheet, hills of blood. Passages to nationhood in Greek Macedonia 1870–1990, The University of Chicago Press 1997, p. 148, http://en.wikipedia.org/wiki/Karamanlides. In may 2006 when I was updating my English book in an entry Karamanlides there was an information that they were an ethnic mixture of Greeks, Persians and Turks. In November 2011 when again I was checking this entry to this book this information was non-existent.

[68] http://en.wikipedia.org/wiki/Greek_refugees

[69] S. Kiselinovski, Etničkite promeni..., p. 45.

Secondly, the expulsion of Christian Macedonians to Bulgaria and Muslim Turks (274.052 in the year of 1913) and Macedonians to Turkey[70]. In the years 1913–1928 89.208 Macedonians were displaced and to Turkey 40.802[71] Forced displacement of populations was a consequence of the Lozanne treaty signed on 23 June 1923.[72,73] The consequence of this treaty was the altering of the ethnic structure. Macedonians became a minority (240.000 in 1913) in Macedonia whereas previously they had been a majority (370.371 in 1913)[74]. and a Greek-speaking minority (236.755 in 1913)[75] ethnically Greek and non-Greek [it regards mainly the Vlah population[76] (Mac. Vlasi, Gr. Vlahi) also called Aromanian speaking Valahian (it is practically a Romanian language which in the Macedonian territory has borrowed many Macedonian words and modern Greek words) but declaring as Greek[77] and being in fact the fifth

---

70 Ibidem, p. 30.

71 S. Kiselinovski, ibidem, p. 41.

72 See the Treaty text at http://wwi.lib.byu.edu/index.php/Treaty_of_Lausanne, T. Triadafilopoulos, The 1923 Greek-Turkish exchange of population and the reformulation of Greek national identity, speech prepared for the conferance *Exchange of Populations Between Greece and Turkey:*

An Assessment of the Consequences of the Treaty of Lausanne took place at the University of Oxford 17–20 September 1998.

73 Historiography has erroneously accused Turkey of the forced exchanges of populations between Greece and Turkey. This is due mainly to the Greek influence over western historiography showing Turkey in bad light. See D. Pentzopoulos, "The Balkan Exchange of minorities and its impact on Greece", pp. 58 and 70. In reality it was the Greek side which arbitrarily forced the exchange of populations on Turkey. The Christian population that lived in Turkey, which was exchanged with Greece, was never asked if it was interested in participating in such an exchange. Recognizing the Christian population as Greek, Greece alone decided for it. Greek author Konstantinos Svolopoulos wrote about this in a book published in 1981 by the Association of Macedonian Studies, cited after G. Nakratzas, "The close racial..." p. 91. See also the treaty text at: http://wwi.lib.byu.edu/index.php/Treaty_of_Lausanne

74 S. Kiselinovski, ibidem, p. 30.

75 Ibidem, p. 26.

76 http://en.wikipedia.org/wiki/Vlah.

77 Thade Kahle is one of the most eminent specialist on the Valahian matters in the Balkans. He divides Valahians into three national orientations. First is Romanian, second is Greek and third is Valahian. In my estimation in the past as

column towards the Macedonians] living in Aegean Macedonia became majority (854.954 altogether)[78]

Between 1923 and 1930 about a million and a quarter of Orthodox Greeks and non-Greeks were sent from Turkey to Greece, and a rather smaller number of Muslim Turks and Macedonians from Greece to Turkey. The Greeks of Karaman who were 'repatriated' to Greece were Greek Christians by religion-yet most of them knew no Greek. Their language was Turkish-which they wrote in the Greek script-and the inscriptions in their abandoned churches and cemeteries in Karaman still testify to their linguistic Turkishness. In the same way, many of the repatriated Turks from Greece knew little or no Turkish, but spoke Greek-and wrote it in the Turco-Arabic script. What took place was not an exchange of Christians and Ottoman Muslims. A Western observer, accustomed to a different system of social and national classification, might even conclude that this was no repatriation at all, but two deportations into exile-of Christian Turks to Greece, and of Muslim Greeks to Turkey[79].

Thirdly, the introduction of anti-Macedonian laws banning the use of the Macedonian language in communication, maintaining and cultivating the Macedonian tradition and folklore. People not obeying the laws were met with high fines and terrorized; terrifying the Macedonian population in order to

---

well at present 80% of Valahians represent the Greek option. See T. Kahl, The ethnicity of Aromanians after 1990: the identity of a minority that behaves like a majority, Ethnologia Balcanica, Vol. 6 (2002), p. 146.

[78] See S. Kiselinovski, Egejskot del na Makedonija 1918–1989, Skopje 1990, pp. 19–42, A. Rossos, os. cit. p. 142.

[79] B. Lewis, The emergence of modern Turkey, Third edition, OUP, 2002, pp. 334–355. It is worth for a reader to get known with the two books of Pavlos Koufis/Pavle Kufev inserted in the bibliography. The books describe the Macedonian language and folklor in Greek Macedonia. The books are written in modern Greek.

abandon its Macedonian character as quickly as possible. It is worth to add that Greece led a very pervasive policy.

From one side it was fighting with all appearances for the Macedonian character in Greece and externally it tried to show herself as a country respecting the minority rights of those who lived on her territory. These minority rights were a result of the Sevres treaty signed on 10 August 1920 in which the Greek government was obliged to protect non-Greek national minorities living in Greece.[80] To satisfy some League of Nations requirements, the Greek government published a primer for the Macedonian children entitled Abecedar. It was prepared by a special commission of experts and linguists, written in the Lerin-Bitola dialect. By doing so the Greek government recognized the existence of Macedonians on its territory. Just after a visit by a League of Nations representative and after viewing the primer, instead of sending the primer to schools in Macedonia, the entire batch was withdrawn from the public and destroyed.[81]

---

80 I , Michailidis, Minority rights and educational problems in Greek interwar Macedonia: the case of the primer „Abecedar"', Journal of Modern Greek Studies, 14/2 (1996), pp. 329–343, J. Shea, Macedonia and Greece: the struggle to define a new Balkan nation, pp. 109–111, McFarland & Co., Inc., Publishers, Jefferson, North Carolina and London 1997. It is worth for a reader to get known with the two books of Pavlos Koufis/Pavle Kufev inserted in the bibliography. The books describe the Macedonian language and folklor in Greek Macedonia. The books are written in modern Greek.

81 On principles of Trotskism, https://en.wikipedia.org/wiki/Trotskyism [download 29.11.2011].

The cover page of the Abecedar. The second page of the Abecedar.

ABECEDAR

ΕΝ ΑΘΗΝΑΙΣ
ΤΥΠΟΙΣ Π. Δ. ΣΑΚΕΛΛΑΡΙΟΥ
1925

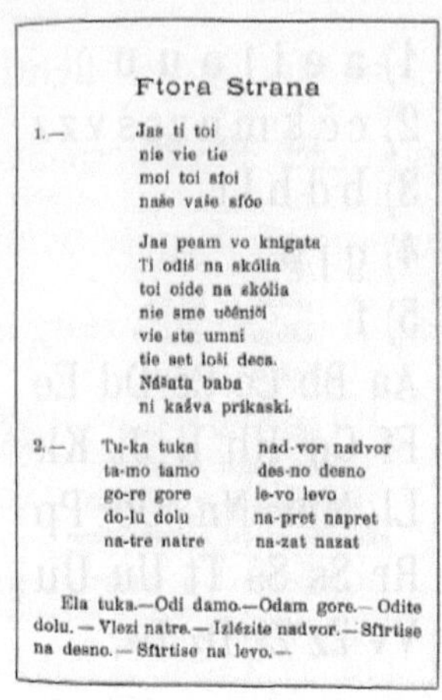

Ftora Strana

1.— Jas ti toi
nie vie tie
moi toi sfoi
naše vaše sfóe

Jas peam vo knigata
Ti odiš na skólia
toi oide na skólia
nie sme učěniči
vie ste umni
tie set loši deca.
Nášata baba
ni kažva prikaski.

2.— Tu-ka tuka	nad-vor nadvor
ta-mo tamo	des-no desno
go-re gore	le-vo levo
do-lu dolu	na-pret napret
na-tre natre	na-zat nazat

Ela tuka.—Odi damo.—Odam gore.—Odite dolu.—Vlezi natre.—Izlézite nadvor.—Sfirtise na desno.—Sfirtise na levo.—

90

Source: http://www.florina.org/abecedar/054.asp [download: 25.11.2012].
Source: http://www.florina.org/abecedar/087.asp[download: 25.11.2012].

Graph 2. Change of ethnic composition in Macedonia 1913-1928

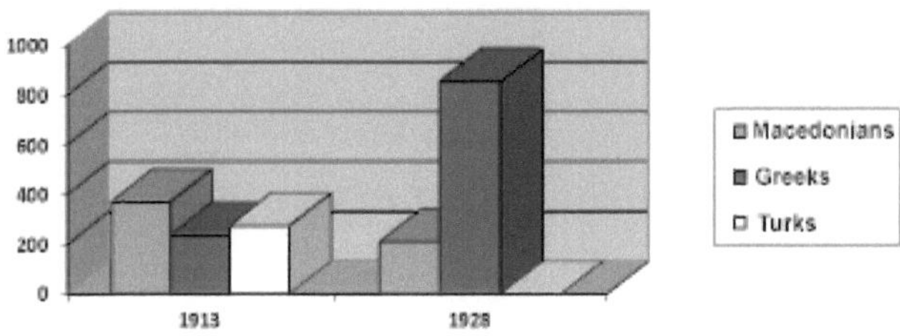

Source: S. Kiselinovski, Etničkite promeni vo Makedonija (1913-1995), Skopje 2000, p. 30 and 45.

This description of the "*Great Idea*" is necessary to understand the stance of the CPG towards Macedonia. Even if the CPG had abandoned the idea, it is none the less true that the model of Greek patriotism accepted by the CPG is derived from it. In effect, the CPG and the "*Great Idea*" are identical. Only after 1924 did a section of the Greek communists distance itself from this concept with the result that they accepted the existence of a distinct Macedonian nationality in Aegean Macedonia (today Northern Greece).

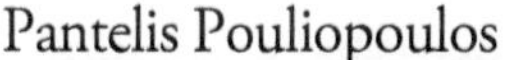

Source: http://en.wikipedia.org/wiki/File:Pantelis_Pouliopoulos.jpg [download 30.11.2011].

Returning to our main theme, however, it is necessary to describe the political and economic situation in Greece in order to appreciate the conditions in which the first Greek Socialists, and later Communists, lived and worked.

As a member of the Entente, Greece received additional territory after the first world war, namely, Epirus, Macedonia including the port of Salonika, and Thrace. But economically Greece was in crisis. There were no developed industries and the Greek market was badly supplied. The lot of the majority of the population was hard. Only the aristocracy and middle classes were better off. In many cases they were able to exploit the difficult situation of the country to enrich themselves, obviously at the expense of the poorer members of society. These included people who, although aware that they were being exploited, seized every opportunity to work. Such was the price exacted to satisfy their basic needs. It regarded mainly the workers. Politically, Greece was not stable. Although the leader of the liberal-national movement, Elevtherios Venizelos, repeated premier, supported of the Greater Greece and the republic thanks to whom Greece received enormous territorial gains[82] in the Neuilly and Sevres treaties and then general Ioannis Metaxas[83] chairman of a party Free Thought declared monarchist[84]and later dictator from 1936 endeavoured to bring it about. The whole Greek political life of 40s of XX century was dominated by the struggle between liberals and monarchists. All this caused that the Socialist movement could develop and gain another successes. The internal situation in Greece was favourable to it.

82 en.wikipedia.org/wiki/Ioannis_Metaxas

83 M. Tanty, Bałkany w XX wieku, Warszawa 2003, p. 202.

84 M. Tanty, Bałkany w XX wieku, Warszawa 2003, p. 202.

Elevtherios Venizelos

Ioannis Metaxas

Source: http://en.wikipedia.org/wiki/File Ελευθέριος_Βενιζέλος.jpg[download: 30.11.2011].
Source: http://en.wikipedia.org/wiki/File:Metaxas.jpg [download: 30.11.2011].

Another view of this situation is provided by G. D. H. Cole in his "*History of Socialist Thought*" (London 1958).[85] In his opinion, parlous economic situations and political instability were not factors conducive to the development of socialism and later communism. The history of the socialist movement in fact suggests the opposite, namely, that difficult economic and political situations actually promoted the acceptance and spread of socialism and communism in Europe. The best example is Germany at the end of the first world war.

The first congress of the one thousand socialist organisations throughout Greece took place at the *Piraeus Hotel* in Athens from 4 to 10 November

[85] See G D H Cole, History of Socialist Thought, Macmillan, London 1958 pp. 282–286.

1918.[86] Its aim was to establish one party to represent the Greek socialists - the "*Socialist Workers Party of Greece*"[87] (Gr. Sosialistikon Erghatikon Komma Elladhas SWPG)[88]. Its founder was a Sephardi Jew[89] Avraam Benaroya[90] born at Vidin in Bulgaria at the family of small merchants. He studied law in Belgrade but he did not finish it. He was a polyglot, commanded six languages. Then he returned to Bulgaria and worked as a teacher at Plovdiv. After the outbreak of the Young Turks revolution[91] in 1908 he left for Salonika as a socialist organizer and remained in it for good. It is worth to add that Salonika was a centre of a revolutionary as well as Masonic activity and most frequently one interwoven with the other.

At its inaugural congress, the SWPG drew attention to the continuing existence of unresolved problems both national and territorial from before the first world war. The SWPG committee, however, charged with the resolution of these matters, was not able to take any decisions which would be unanimously accepted. Only the inaugural congress could do this.[92] Thus two groups of socialists emerged; the so-called "*reformists*" (N Yaniou, A Sidheris) and those who opposed them on the left (D Lighdhopoulos, N Komiotis, Tzoulatis). The inaugural congress passed two resolutions; the "*Minority*

---

86 R Kirjazovski, KPG i makedonskoto nacionalno prašanje 1918–1974, Skopje 1982, p. 4. Documents show that the Congress took place from 4 to 10 November 1948. See also D G Kousoulas, Revolution and Defeat, London 1965, p. 1.

87 D G Kousoulas, os. cit p. 2.

88 http://en.wikipedia.org/wiki/Sephardi_Jews, http://en.wikipedia.org/wiki/History_of_the_Jews_of_Thessaloniki.

89 http://en.wikipedia.org/wiki/Avraam_Benaroya.

90 http://en.wikipedia.org/wiki/Young_Turk_Revolution.

91 Ilicak, H. Şükrü (September 2002). Jewish socialism in Ottoman Salonica. Southeast European and Black Sea Studies 2 (3): pp.115–146.

92 S Kiselinovski, os. cit. p. 59.

Resolution" represented by the reformists and the "*Minority Resolution*" put forward by the left representing mostly members of the Greek Workers' Movement.[93]

Below I analyse the contents of both these resolutions concerning the national and territorial disputes existing in Europe after the end of the first world war.

The Minority Resolution.

"Our views concerning all current international disputes are as follows; all European disputes such as those of Alsace, Poland, Triest etc may be solved in accordance with the Wilson programme whose main points have been agreed to be Europe's workers. We probably share the same views as workers in other countries although we are not acquainted with the details. Greek workers know at first hand the problems of the Balkans and the eastern Mediterranean and are thus best qualified to express an opinion about them. Accordingly we make the following demands;

1. European Turkey to become an autonomous republic occupying both shores of the Sea of Marmara. The Straits of Marmara to become international and, like the Autonomous Republic of Thrace, to be placed under the protection of the League of Nations.

2. Bulgarian Thrace to be annexed to the Autonomous Republic of Thrace. [which later being already Greek, the former would then also become part of Greece]

[93] ibid. p. 59.

3. Greece never to lay claim to Bitola and Serbia to recognise that Salonika belongs to Greece.

4. The creation of an independent Albania outside the spheres of influence of Austria, Italy, Serbia and Greece.

5. Italy to withdraw from Valona which is to be recognised by Albania except for Northern Epirus which should be ceded to Greece.

6. Recognition of the right of Romania to Dobrudža and Transylvania and of the Serbs to Bosnia Herzegovina. The Yugoslavs to create separate, independent states and Bessarabia to become independent but as part of the Soviet State. [This concept of the "widest frontiers" was proposed by the USSR - footnote in the document] In this way it would escape the excessively expansionist policies of Serbia and Romania at the expense of other Balkan states.

7. The creation of a pan-Balkan Democratic Federation.

8. In Asia, the areas of Smyrna and Aydin from the northern frontier of the Autonomous State of Thrace to the eastern and southern frontiers of Asiatic Turkey to be ceded to Greece.

9. Italy to be denied its claim to Atalia which should be given to Turkey to grant it access to the sea.

10. The Dodecanese to be returned to Greece.

11. Syria from its northern and eastern frontiers with Turkey and its southern frontier with Israel to be ceded to France.

12. The Old Town in Jerusalem to be part of the independent Republic of Israel.

13. Southern Palestine to be ceded to Great Britain.

14. A Republic of the Sea of Marmara to be created on the southern shore of the Black Sea bounded to the east by Soviet Russia and to the south by Turkey and Armenia.

15. An independent republic of Armenia to be created in Asia Minor on Armenian territory.

16. Turkey to form a free republic in the centre of Asia Minor with free access to the sea at the port of Alexandretta. "[94]

The *Minority Resolution* appeared on 12 November 1918 in the journal "*Rizospastis*" (The Radical) which was soon to become the official organ of the CPG. It is clear that the "*Minority*" stood for self-determination, for example, of Alsace, Poland and Triest. On the solution of national and territorial problems, the "*Minority*" supported policies favourable to Greece. The first point of the Resolution concerning European Turkey mentions Eastern Thrace which would become the Autonomous Republic of Marmara straddling both shores of the Sea of Marmara. In effect, this would become a Greek mini-state. The Bosphorus, linking Istanbul with the Republic of Turkey, that is the Republic of Marmara, would come under the protection of the League of Nations. This state would thus find itself between the rivers Mesta amd Maritsa. The population of this territory was Greek. The Communists, with the interests of the state and the Greek people in mind, wished to establish an independent mini-state which would in future be

[94] R Kirjazovski, KPG i makedonskoto nacionalno prašanje, Skopje, 1982, pp. 6–7.

annexed to Greece proper, thus achieving both independence from Turkey and a weakening of the Turkish state.

In the second point concerning Bulgarian Thrace, the *Minority Resolution* proposed the annexation of Western Thrace together with the Republic of Thrace.[95] The third point concerns the ending of the Greek-Serbian dispute as well as the status of Bitola and Salonika. Both parties wished to come to an agreement in order to ensure no territorial changes, i.e. to uphold the status quo, particularly as Greece wished to retain Salonika for access to the sea. In the fourth point, there is a very deliberate attempt to establish an independent state of Albania. The Albanians were both Muslims and Christians and so creating a Muslim state would lead to conflicts which Greece could exploit to its own advantage.[96] The fifth point was also cunningly thought out. Italy was to withdraw from Valona and Greece would receive in exchange (for nothing) Northern Epirus, non-Greek territory[97] but of vital strategic interest because it would afford access to the Adriatic. The sixth point was very advantageous to Greece. By recognising Romanian claims to Dobrudža, territory belonging ethnically to Bulgaria, it would provoke conflict between two countries which would weaken both of them to the advantage of Greece. Transylvania was disputed territory between Hungary and Romania. A further proposal in point six would also be advantageous to Greece. The annexation of Bessarabia, ethnically Romanian and part of the USSR would cause friction between the

[95] S Kiselinovski in the notes of his book, p. 60 explains that at the Peace Conference Western Thrace was joined to Greece but the "Minority" did not know this. Hence in the Resolutions, reference is made to Western Thrace in the Republic of Marmara.

[96] ibid.

[97] See chapter one of this book.

two states, weakening Romania and strengthening the Soviet Union. In Asia Minor, so-called Anatolia, the Minority Resolution demanded Smyrna and Aydin. The Dodecanese would also fall to Greece (see point ten). Furthermore, the Minority Resolution also mentioned establishing an independent Armenian Republic. The Armenians were the natural enemy of the Turks and so Greece would emerge in a stronger position vis-a-vis her ancient Turkish foe (see point fifteen).

Point twelve mentions the creation of an independent Israeli state including Jerusalem. This proposal completely ignores the interests of the Arabs even though they lived in Jerusalem. However, the proposal was made because the "*Minority*" wished to expel Jews living in Salonika and recognising an Israeli state appeared to be the best way of doing this. The Greek middle classes showed considerable interest in the wealth which would thus fall into their hands.[98] As is evident, the "*Minority*" programme was not so much socialist as nationalist.[99]

The "*Majority Resolution*" adopted a different tack.

The Majority Resolution

1. To open negotiations for a general peace without annexation or reparations and on the basis of the rights of the people, all warring nations including Russia to be included and all previous agreements annulled.

2. Representatives of the working class of different countries chosen by the organisers to participate in the negotiations.

---

[98] S Kiselinovski, os. cit. p. 61.

[99] S Kiselinovski, os. cit. p. 2.

3. All warring and neutral countries to accept the following conditions essential for a lasting peace;

a) immediate withdrawal of all armies from various countries, disclosure of all secret treaties and cessation of all secret diplomacy.

b) suspension of military service and substitution of a militia for a regular army.

c) immediate demobilisation and disarmament and demolition of all fortifications and bases.

d) all seas to be accessible internationally and all straits to be opened.

e) all factories producing military equipment to be placed under international control and changed to non-military production.

f) recognition of all nations and peoples, irrespective of size, with full rights defined by their own systems of government.

g) all national and territorial disputes to be decided by plebiscite without foreign interference.

h) colonial problems to be solved on the same conditions.

4. Dissolve current alliances and create a League of Nations to guarantee their respective independence.

5. An International Customs Union and an International Committee to be the political and economic basis of the League.

The Socialist Workers Party of Greece considers that to achieve the above aims, it is necessary to convene immediately an International Congress of Socialists whose decision will be binding on all members.

Balkan Disputes

In order to settle Balkan disputes, particularly in so far as they concern our country, the Congress proposes;

1. granting full independence to the islands of Cyprus, Imbros, Limnos, Tenedhos, Samothrace, the Dodecanese and Castellorizo (Castelrosso) as well as Northern Epirus so that they may determine their own status.

2. granting full rights of return and the payment of compensation to all refugees forced from their homes in Balkan countries and Asia Minor, irrespective of their nationality. Furthermore, the means for their return are to be provided.

3. transforming the present area into a federation comprising the vilayets on democratic lines so that peoples from the east would become an independent Commonwealth and thus form part of the Democratic Balkan Federation.

4. Concerning other Balkan questions, the Congress resolved the following;

Establishment of a Democratic Balkan Federation.The Congress of the Socialist Workers Party of Greece, convened at Piraeus 4-10 November 1918 predicts the following;

- *the class struggle carried on by the Balkan proletariat will become more acute in response to the foreign policies of the Balkan countries and the Super Powers.*
- *the economic, political and social development of the Balkan countries will restrain the ruling classes who strive for political hegemony at the expense of their neighbours, thus weakening their own countries.*

- *as a result of these internal developments, the reactionary policies of the Super Powers will complement their external policies towards the Balkans which are of considerable interest to them because of their wealth and geographical position.*
- *the policies of the Super Powers, their influence and acquisition [of territory] will facilitate the break up of the Balkan peninsula into numerous small states, vassals of the Super Powers, who will exploit their desire for hegemony and make them pliant tools [of the Super Powers].*
- *the dynastic and Royalist-Fascist system will foster growth of nationalistic egoism and political intrigue and will support military actions (adventurism).*

independence, social progress and even the security of the Balkan people themselves will be endangered if they do not unite to defend the values of progress and civilisation.

- *as history has shown in relation to the heterogeneous ethnic nature of the Balkan people, it is not possible to solve these problems by force of arms which simply complicates matters and maintains the status quo which serves only the aims of the imperialists.*

The Socialist Workers Party of Greece considers that socialist parties in the Balkans are obliged to;

1. *Oppose all political claims of the imperialist forces concerning unsolved problems because they stir up hatred and destroy confidence which may lead to future wars.*
2. *Oppose every alliance of those Balkan peoples wishing to attain to the rights and freedoms of other Balkan peoples because this would lead to catastrophe*

instead of solidarity and friendships. Without recognising territorial changes as a means to solving Balkan disputes, the parties should proclaim that the sole route to the union of the Balkan peoples is the establishment of a Democratic Balkan Federation on the basis of a radical democracy which would guarantee full and lawful political participation, national and linguistic freedoms irrespective of race or creed and which would have a legislative body and local parliaments with free and direct elections on the basis of proportional representation, enforced by a militia.

In order to realise the above aims, the Congress proposes as a first step the immediate formation of a Post, Telegraph and Customs union and a political and economic alliance of Balkan countries opposed to any foreign intervention or influence; furthermore, the convening of a Pan-Balkan Socialist Workers Congress with the aim of working out a common policy for the working classes of the Balkans towards a renewal of the Pan-Balkan Socialist Bureau. "

Comparing the two resolutions, we note that from the beginning, the first one mentions the need for negotiations, thanks to which world peace had been established. All warring nations should take part in these talks. Besides the governments of these countries, representatives of the working class [see paragraph 2] should also participate in these talks. This declaration was crucial because probably for the first time representatives of the working class would be able jointly to participate in the new post-war Soviet order which they would otherwise not have been able to. Paragraph 3 concerns the conditions under which peace could be guaranteed in the future. Some of these paragraphs however ignored reality and could not be realised. These included the demands for the publication of all secret agreements and the abandonment of all secret diplomacy. Similarly for paragraph c concerning complete disarmament and destruction of military bases. Equally futile was paragraph e. Other sub-paragraphs of paragraph 3 and the first part of sub-paragraph a and c and sub-paragraphs f and g were reasonable. Similarly for paragraphs 4 and 5. Concerning Balkan affairs, the "*Majority Resolution*", in contrast to the "*Minority*" demanded liberty and rights of self-determination for the populations of the islands of Cyprus, Imbros, Limnos, Tenedhos, Samothraki, the Dodecanese and Castellorizo (Castelrosso) as well as for Northern Epirus (Southern Albania).

Map 4. Disputed islands between Greece and Turkey.

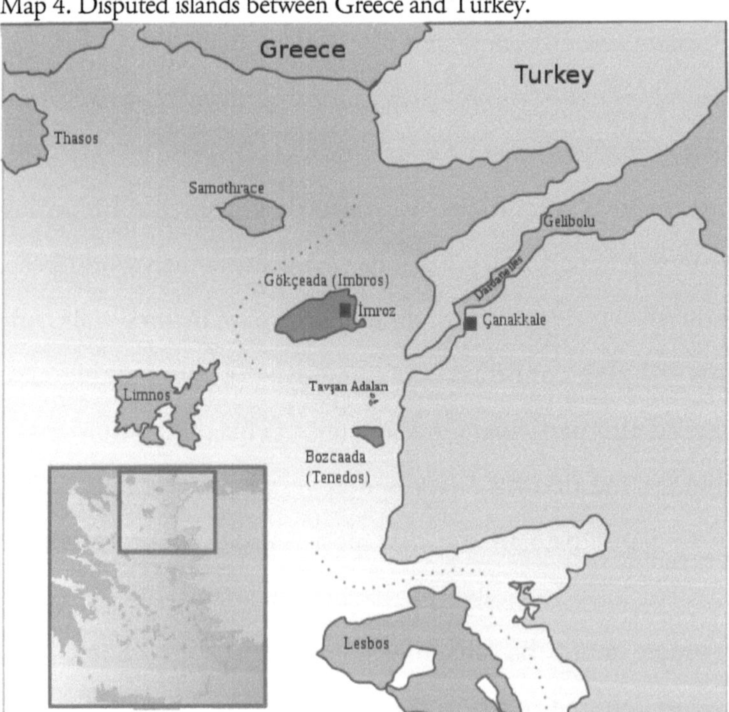

Source: http://pl.wikipedia.org/w/index.php?title=Plik:ImbrosTenedos_2.svg&filetimestamp=20070130063328 [download: 30.11.2011].

Paragraph 2 demanded the right of repatriation of all refugees from other Balkan countries and Asia Minor and mentioned the possibility of financial assistance. Paragraph 3 mentioned the establishment of a Balkan Federation based on democratic principles. The reasons for Balkan underdevelopment were ascribed to the ruling classes. The Super Powers were seen as the major exploiters of the wealth of the Balkans. The "*Minority*" adopted a contrasting approach by calling for unity within a Balkan Federation. In this way the problems of all peoples on foreign territories would be automatically resolved. National freedoms and languages, irrespective of race or creed would be guaranteed.

Of the two resolutions put forward to solve the Balkans' pressing problems, the "*Majority Resolution*"[100] was carried at the SWRG Congress. Both resolutions however had much in common. Both suggested answers to questions posed by the Dodecanese, Cyprus, Northern Epirus [or preferable, Southern Albania] and Aegean Macedonia. Greece was keenly interested in all these questions.

The policy of the "*Majority*" towards the unsolved problems of nationalities and territories was as follows;

[100] S Kiselinovski, os. cit. p. 61.

Graph 3. Ethnic composition of Dodekanez in 1918

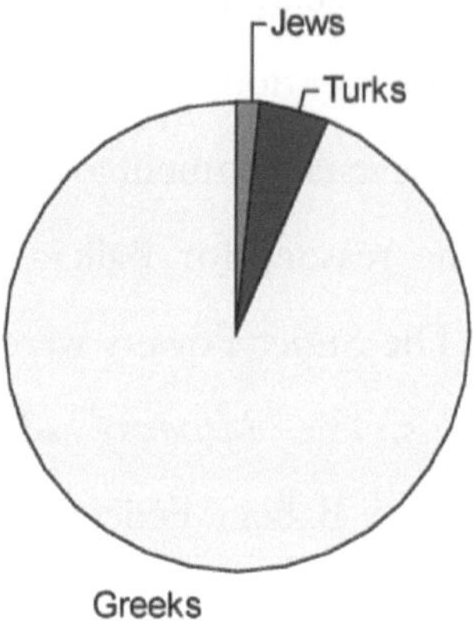

Source:S. Kiselinovski, *Egejskiot del na Makedonija(1918-1989)*, Skopje 1990, p. 57.

Ethnically Greek territories, i.e. the Dodecanese and Cyprus, formally under foreign control, should have the right of self-determination. This demand was made because Greece envisaged the annexation of these territories given that the majority of the inhabitants were actually Greek. Statistically, in the Dodecanese 131,761 people (93.5% of the population) were Greek, 6874 (4.8%) Turkish and 2455 (1.7%) Jewish. The total population was 143,090 in 1918. (See graph on page 28).

It is thus clear from the statistics that those wishing to unite with Greece were justified. Both '*ius solis*' (rights to historical territory) and '*ius civitas*' (rights of settlement) were in favour of the Greeks. The Turks were a minority, 14.35% of the whole population and lived on territory both ethnically and historically foreign to them.[101]

---

101 S Kiselinovski, os. cit. p. 62.

In Cyprus, 274,180 people (79.9%) were Greek, 64,180 ((18.65%) Turkish and 5666 (1.65%) were of mixed origin.[102] (See graph below).

Graph 4.Ethnic composition of Cyprus in 1918

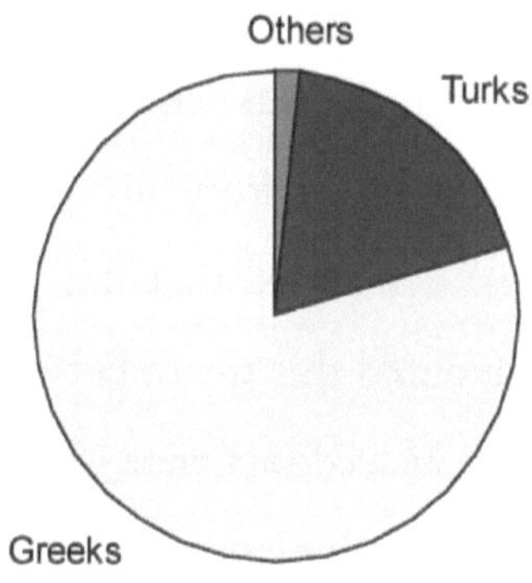

Source:S. Kiselinovski, *Egejskiot del na Makedonija(1918-1989)*, Skopje 1990, p.57.

Albanian territory, more specifically its modern Southern part, was inhabited by 40,000 people of Greek origin, comprising 17% of the population. Both '*ius solis*' and '*ius civitas*' (rights of the Christian and Muslim Albanians comprising 83% of the population) would lay the foundations of a new Albanian state.[103] The Greeks would retain their rights of language, culture and nationality as a minority living in Albania. But despite these obvious facts, the "*Majority Resolution*" demanded that the Greek minority, comprising only 17% of the population and living on territory both historically and ethnically foreign, be granted the right of self-determination,

[102] Meghali Elliniki Enkiklopedia, Athina 1930, vol. 4, p. 600 in S Kiselinovski os. cit.

[103] J Ancel, Peuples et Nations des Balkans, Paris 1930, p. 185 in Kiselinovski os. cit.

thus in effect constituting annexation by Greece.[104] However, the most important problem which Greece faced both after the Balkan wars and the first world war was that of Macedonia. The vast majority of the population of Aegean Macedonia (now Northern Greece) was of non-Greek origin (as much as 77.5%) and lived on territory which was ethnically and historically Macedonian.[105] Both '*ius civitas*' (right of territory historically Macedonian) and '*ius solis*' (rights of Macedonians) demanded that this problem be treated as a Macedonian one. Two factors favoured this treatment despite the fact that only 22% of the population in Aegean Macedonia were Greek, the SWPG was not consistent in its handling of the Macedonian question. If we compare its demands for the self-determination of various peoples with the lack of any such demand for the Macedonians (comprising a majority of 77.5%) or for Albanians in Southern Albania (83%) as well as Western Thrace, then this is tantamount to an endorsement by the SWPG of the "*Great Idea*" which automatically rejects the rights of all non-Greeks. The SWPG considered Aegean Macedonia as an inherent part of Greece, ignoring the rights of the Macedonians to their historical territory (*ius civitas*) and their declarations on the matter,[106] the SWPG stated that the Macedonian problem had been solved. Up to 1924 the Macedonian question was of little interest to the SWPG. Only in 1924 were they forced to take decisions, not because they wanted to but because of the new situation in which they found themselves. The "*Resolutions*" began to reflect the official views of the Greek authorities.

---

104 S Kiselinovski, os. cit. p. 63.

105 ibid.

106 ibid. p. 64.

The "*Great Idea*" began to be understood as "*Greater Greece*" and decisions taken about non-Greek territories (Aegean Macedonia, Southern Albania, Western Thrace) offer indisputable proof of this. But the greatest and most pressing problem, the Macedonian national problem, remained.[107]

[107] ibid. p. 65.

CHAPTER

3

THE CPG AND ITS POLICY OF "STATEHOOD WITHOUT NATIONHOOD" 1924–31

From the very beginning, the CPG consistently denied the existence of a Macedonian problem which had in fact arisen in 1918 when Aegean Macedonia was annexed by Greece. If the question arose at all, it was treated as an internal matter. It was due only to the insistence of the International Communist Movement and the Balkan Communist Federation that Macedonia ceased to be a matter for Greece alone but was placed firmly on the Balkan agenda.

In the spring of 1921 a delegation of the CPG went to Moscow to take part in the III Congress of the International Communist Movement — the Comintern.[108] The CPG had changed its name from the Socialist Workers Party of Greece which it called itself at the II Congress in Athens on 5 April 1920. They had then decided to take part in the III Congress of the Comintern[109] and sent a delegation led by Gheorghios Gheorghiadhis. In Moscow for the first time the CPG had to adopt a position on the question of

108 G Kousoulas, Revolution and Defeat. The Story of the Greek Communist Party. OUP London 1965, p. 54.

109 ibid. p. 4.

autonomy for Aegean Macedonia at the instigation of Vasil Kolarov, future secretary of the Communist Party of Bulgaria (CPB). Gheorghiadhis expressed astonishment and refused to give any undertaking.[110] The Politburo of the CPB brought the matter up again in May 1922 when Kolarov demanded autonomy for Macedonia and requested backing from other Communist Parties. But Yanis Petsopoulos rejected the demand[111] and requested that the matter be postponed until the next meeting of the Central Committee of the CPG — after their return to Greece of course. The question was raised again in 1923 at a conference of the BCF in Sofia. A spokesman for the CPG, A. Stavridhis, resisted pressure brought on him by the conference saying "*The policy of a united and independent Macedonia is not acceptable to the Greek colonisers [people settled in Aegean Macedonia by the Greek authorities] who are a majority there, nor does it interest political emigres in Bulgaria whose government is more interested in uniting Macedonia with Bulgaria*".[112]

The Macedonian question arose again at a meeting of the BCF which was convened after the defeat of the September uprising in Bulgaria. The uprising had been directed against the bourgeois government of Tsankov but the party had remained neutral, the insurgents lacked co-ordination and as a result the uprising had failed.[113] A meeting of the BCF took place in Moscow where

---

110 ibid. p. 54.

111 See G Kousoulas, os. cit. Despite the merits of this book, tracing the his tory of the CPG from the revolution to 1949, it is too one-sided and the events are seen from a Greek perspective which vitiates its account of the Macedonian national problem. The author presents the views of the "minority" in the CPG and accepts the postulate of the "Great Idea". Like the author of the book "The Greek Tragedy", Constantine Tsoucalas, he considers the CPG's handling of the Macedonian problem was a major political error.

112 K A Bramu, Slavokomunistikes oraghanosis en Makedhonias. Athina 1969. p. 86 in S Kiselinovski, Egejskiot del na Makedonija 1918–1989, Skopje 1980, p. 66.

113 See further in T Wasilewski. Historia Bułgarii, Wrocław 1988, pp. 247—250.

Georgi Dimitrov and Vasil Kolarov again urged the acceptance of the slogan "*A United and Independent Macedonia*". The representative of the CPG, N. Sarghologhos, however, refused to accept their arguments.[114]

Georgi Dimitrov

Vasil Kolarov

Source: http://en.wikipedia.org/wiki/File:Georgi_Dimitrov.jpg[download: 30.11.2011]
Source: http://en.wikipedia.org/wiki/File:V.kolarov.jpg[download: 30.11.2011]

Like his predecessor, Stavridhis, he maintained that this slogan was not acceptable to the CPG, particularly after the forced exchange of populations between Greece and Turkey and the mass settlement of Greeks in Aegean Macedonia.[115] This exchange of populations occurred after the signing of an agreement between Greece and Turkey in Lausanne in 1923. Christians were moved to Greece [some of them were Greek-speaking Greeks but others were Turkish-speaking Christians] and Muslims moved to Turkey [they were both

[114] S Kiselinovski os. cit. p. 66.

[115] N A Hristoforou. To Makedhoniko zitima kai i sovietiki politiki. Thessaloniki 1954, p. 112 in S Kiselinovski, os. cit. p. 66.

Turks and Muslim Macedonians].[116] However at the V Congress of the Comintern in Moscow in 1924, the CPG was severely criticised by the leader of the Comintern and expert on Balkan affairs, Dmitriy Manuilskiy as well as Vasil Kolarov, chairman of the BCF for "*Austro-Marxism*". The CPG recognised a "*United and Independent Macedonia*" in theory but refused to accept it in practice.[117] Kolarov's arguments were supported by Manuilskiy who declared that "*in Greek, Serbian, Bulgarian and Albanian Macedonia there live a people who, independently of the ethnic diversity about them, have nurtured their own Macedonian historical traditions and are thus entitled to the unwritten law of national independence and sovereignty*".[118]

Predictably the CPG was reluctant to accept these facts. The Greek delegate at the V Conference of the Comintern, Serafim Maximos, disputed the arguments of Kolarov and Manuilskiy. He said that the policy of a "*United and Independent Macedonia was not acceptable to the CPG because more than 700,000 Greek refugees and workers now lived there and they were not disposed to accept Macedonian autonomy*".[119]

---

[116] See H Batowski, Państwa Bałkańskie 1800-1923, Kraków 1938 p. 273.

[117] See V Kartov, Makedonskiot narod i pravoto na samoopredeluvanje 1912-1941 Skopje 1987, p. 447. The particular merit of this book is that it offers a balanced history of the Macedonian national struggle for self-determination in an historical perspective.

[118] G D Katsouli, Istoria tou KKE, tom 11, 192–327. Athina 1976, pp. 140–141 in S Kiselinovski os. cit. p. 66.

[119] A G Elefantis, I Apeghelia tis adhinatis epanastasis. Athina 1976, p. 38 in S Kiselinovski, os. cit.

Dimitriy Manuilskiy

en.wikipedia.org/wiki/Dmitry_Manuilsky[download: 30.11.2011].

In the face of intense pressure, the Greek delegates at the V Congress, Serafim Maximos, Pantelis Pouliopoulos and N Meghas, accepted the declaration of the Comintern and BCF on Macedonia. The best description of the feelings and attitudes of the Greek communists towards Macedonia appeared in an article by Serafim Maximos published in "*Rizospastis*" on 6 February 1927 entitled "*An Explanation*".

Logo Rizospastis.

Source: http://www1.rizospastis.gr/ [download: 30.11.2011].

"I was a delegate of the Party (together with Pouliopoulos) at the V Congress of the Comintern. I well remember how Comrade Kolarov attacked the Serbian delegate (a Macedonian by origin) who had asked a question about autonomy. "We" he said "are not autonomists. We are communists and as such we ask this question". The Comintern delegate spoke in the same vein. [This was Manuilskiy] I explained how the Macedonian problem is regarded and how our Party became embroiled in a coup for contentious or similar reasons. As representatives of the Party, we received orders to defend what in my opinion were divergent views and convictions. This we eventually did. But as a participant at the Congress I heard, discussed and accepted justifiable views buttressed by facts. I consider it greatly mistaken when some Party warriors express their disappointment about what they consider to be erroneous and destructive policies but which were in fact not only utterly right but powerfully supportive of the revolution".[120]

Maximos' words precisely reflect the views of the majority of the Greek communists, the minority fraction, concerning Macedonia. The resolution of the Macedonian question was accepted because the majority fraction considered it to be the best way to incite revolution in the Balkans. It was of course predictable that accepting this resolution by the Comintern, the BCF and the CPG would cause "*concern among members of the CPG*"[121] because this policy "*did not reflect the wishes or points of view of the Greek communists*".[122] The first hostile reaction came from Yanis Kordhatos , director of the Party

[120] R Kirjazovski, KPG i makedonskoto nacionalno prašanije 1918-1974, Skopje 1982 p. 34.

[121] K Bramou, os. cit. p. 92 in S Kiselinovski os. cit. p. 67.

[122] A Elefantis, I Apeghelia tis adhinatis epinastasis, Athina 1976, p. 38 in S Kiselinovski os. cit. p. 67.

newspaper "*Rizospastis*" and member of the Central Committee of the CPG who wrote;

"The policy of a united and independent Macedonia and Thrace is totally irrelevant [meaning unreal] because Macedonia is divided into three parts and all the inhabitants of Greek Macedonia are Greeks, a fact I can personally vouch for."[123]

Yanis Kordhatos

Source:
https://www.google.pl/search?q=κορδατος+ιωαννης&source=lnms&tbm=isch&sa=X&ved=0ahUKEwirq5X07OfJAhXMvRoKHSQJD [download: 19.12.2015].

The CPG realised that the whole question of Macedonia caused feelings to run deep amidst the rank and file of the Party. Moreover there was strong

[123] K A Bramou, Ibid. p. 92 in S Kiselinovski ibid.

resistance to any positive resolution of the problem. The Party leadership despatched an officer to gauge the mood at grass roots level in order to prepare for the inevitable questions at the next Party congress. As expected, the officer reported negative feelings. All regional parties in Greece expressed their opposition to the policy of the Comintern towards Macedonia.[124] There were only two exceptions; the Party organisation in Piraeus and the Young Communists of Greece (strictly speaking only some of them). Despite this negative reaction, the Macedonian national question was placed on the agenda of the *Extraordinary Congress* of the CPG held in Athens from 26 November to 4 December 1924.[125]

At this congress, an attempt to solve the Macedonian problem along the lines envisaged by the Comintern met with "*prolonged and fierce arguments*"[126] among the rank and file of the Greek communists. In the course of these heated discussions, two main standpoints began to emerge. The first one was a call for a new "*minority*" within the CPG led by Yanis Kordhatos and Thomas Apostolidhis whose aim would be to bring about by any means united and independent Macedonia. The second one called for the formation of a "*majority*" under Pantelis Pouliopoulos and favoured the acceptance of the Comintern's view of the Macedonian question. Kordhatos himself explained his negative stance towards Macedonia in an article published in "*Rizospastis*" on 18 February 1927. Kordhatos referred to the Bulletin of the CPG of 2 May 1926 which published a message from the Central Committee of the

124 S Kiselinovski os. cit. p. 67.

125 V Kartov, os. cit. p. 448.

126 A A Kirou, Sinomasia enandhion tis Makedhonias, Athina 1950, p. 14 in S Kiselinovski ibid. p. 68.

Comintern. This he considered the best exposition of his own views of Macedonia and why he agreed with it.

"We proclaim as a basic principle the right of the minorities in Macedonia and Thrace to self-determination and oppose the oppression of the people ... But this problem is not central to the policies of our Party. If such a minority fights for self-determination on its own, we, as their allies, will help them in their struggle. The struggles of [national] minorities are just. As their allies the CPG will support the Macedonian and Thracian minorities in their struggles provided these struggles continue. We will not provide means to create a movement amongst the minorities in Macedonia or Thrace nor solve their problems for it must not be forgotten that the bourgeois elements in these minorities have interests which conflict with those of the proletariat. We are not basically a Party of national minorities but a Party of the proletariat. The Comintern will aid national liberation movements of people against colonialism provided the mass of the people together with their leaders fight for self-determination. The Comintern will not create national liberation movements at grass roots level who are fighting to realise the aims of paragraphs in their various Resolutions. We, the CPG, shall fight for the rights of national self-determination and against national oppression in Macedonia and Thrace. But the Party as presently constituted must not make the national problem central to our role of political struggle or use slogans such as "Independence for Macedonia and Thrace" as a call to action. Remember that the Communist Party supports national liberation movements but does not directly create them nor shoulder their problems".[127]

---

[127] R Kirjazovski, os. cit. p. 39.

Kordhatos went on to quote Stalin who had assumed the leadership of the Comintern on Lenin's death. His speech to the Yugoslav delegation, according to Kordhatos in the same article "*put things into perspective*". He quotes Stalin as follows;

"In order to avoid any misunderstanding, I must confine myself to this particular problem. The right to independence cannot be understood as a debt owed to oppressed people. Certain comrades, misunderstanding this right, consider that Croatia is "obliged" to seek independence from Yugoslavia. But this is a mistake. Do the same conditions prevail in Macedonia, now under Greek rule? Does a small, defined minority exist which demands the establishment of a separate state? Are not the problems of minorities and of Macedonia under Greek rule the same as those in Southern Serbia, Croatia or Bulgaria? Did there not exist at this time a revolutionary situation in the whole of the Balkans and especially in Macedonia under Greek rule and also in Thrace? This is the truth and nothing but the truth. This is how the problem must be understood and not in the way it has been done at the Congress. On the contrary, it has been turned on its head. It is considered that the Balkans have been set ablaze by revolutionary forces and national minorities. This is a fundamental error, (the first error of the CPB) from which a whole chain of errors has sprung. This is revolutionary adventurism. This mistake must not be covered up when the time comes to judge the CPB. Did not the CPB commit one of its gravest errors on 9 June 1923 and subsequently?"[128]

Kordhatos very adroitly availed himself both of the Comintern's communiques and those of Stalin. In his article, he quotes part of Stalin's

---

[128] ibid. p. 40.

declaration to the effect that the Comintern supports first of all the revolutionary movements and only secondly rights to independence. All this was true except that the Comintern slightly changed its tactics after the death of Lenin when Stalin took over. Kordhatos quoted him from the declaration. However, this declaration was published in 1925, after Lenin's death the previous year. Lenin himself declared that the revolutionary movement can progress only when the rights of peoples to self-determination have been recognised. Only then can Communism be accepted as the ruling system. The next phase after the recognition of the rights of nations, small or large, to self-determination is then the creation of a communist national state within one united Soviet republic,[129] a supranational entity.

Returning to Stalin's declaration, we note that it breaks new ground in his approach to revolutionary matters. In quoting him, Kordhatos does not mention that the revolutionary fervour, which actually existed, was not exploited but dampened down by himself among others. All revolutionary actions in Greece were discouraged unless they were carried out by Greek revolutionaries. No other minority had the right to demonstrate. The reason was simple. The revolution existed to serve only one covert end, that of "*Greater Greece*", allowing Greece to expand into territory which was ethnically non-Greek and to transform old ruling bourgeois regimes into new, communist ones. Returning again to Kordhatos's quotation from the above declaration, it is worth considering an extract from the Proclamation of the

---

129 See further V I Lenin, O Prawie Narodów do Samookreślenia, Warszawa 1952 also J Kowalski, W Lamentowicz, P Wieczorek, Teoria Państwa i Prawa, Warszawa 1983 pp. 471—472, R Tokarczyk, Współczesne doktryny polityczne, Lublin 1984, pp. 52–53.

Executive Committee of the CPG of 25 January 1925 on the death of Lenin. The CPG categorically declared its stance to Lenin's policy on national issues;

"Lenin proclaimed and actively supported the rights of oppressed peoples to self-determination together with secession from the countries in which they lived. No bourgeois party in Greece wishes to heed the words of *Lenin, words with which the Party demands the cessation of attempts to buy off the peoples of Macedonia and Thrace. Let them fight for their own unity and independence. The parties of Greek, Bulgarian, Serbian and Turkish plutocrats know that if Lenin's ideas of national liberation take root, they will lose control of Macedonia and Thrace which they have carved up between them as the spoils of war. Bourgeois parties will brand the Communists as traitors and claim they have sold out the interests of the people and delivered them into the hands of foreign capitalists.*"[130]

Comparing this document with the one quoted by Kordhatos we note that they are diametrically opposed. The one published immediately after the death of Lenin contains his views of the national question while the earlier quoted Comintern document presents a somewhat watered down version of them. Stalin's influence was no doubt the cause of this.

After long and acrimonious discussion, both for and against accepting the concept of a united and independent Macedonia, the matter was put to the vote. 19 delegates voted; 17 voted for the acceptance of the Comintern's proposal for a united and independent Macedonia. Only two voted against — Kordhatos and Apostolidhis, representing the "*Minority*." Despite opposition, the "*Majority*" took the decision at the Third Extraordinary Congress on 3

---

[130] R Kirjazovski, os. cit. p. 25.

December 1924. For the first time in the history of the CPG, a decision was taken about the Macedonian national problem.[131] The text of this historic resolution, entitled "*Independence for Macedonia and Thrace*" is as follows;

"In order to achieve their aims, the Capitalist Powers have never hesitated to use military and economic weapons or to shed the blood of the toiling masses. We need only look at Asia Minor, the Balkans and the Ukraine. They hold us fettered at arm and leg, constantly exposed to all manner of exploitation at the hands of the European bourgeoisie while ensuring their own security. In the Balkans and Asia Minor, the bourgeoisie are preparing themselves for aggressive actions. They are constantly building up their armed strength; three-quarters of their budgets are earmarked for military equipment, weaponry and officer training. Three quarters of their "Loans for Emigrants" [money for Greek refugees from Bulgaria and Turkey settled in Aegean Macedonia in 1924 for whom the Greek authorities demanded and received the sum of £ 12,300,000. - footnote in the document] are used for the same purpose, the death of the refugees. They oppress national minorities in Macedonia and Thrace and plot new wars in the Balkans. Together with the bourgeoisie of Bulgaria and Serbia they sew hatred among peoples and seek their destruction.

By means of intrigue and "national" propaganda, the bourgeoisie seeks to occupy the whole of Macedonia. The Bulgarian bloodsucker Tsankov demands access to Kavala [town in Aegean Macedonia] while the Serbian reactionary Pašič and the royalist-military clique thirst for Salonika. A new imperialist war is about to be unleashed on the Balkans. The Greek bourgeoisie has gathered 700,000

[131] S Kiselinovski, ibid. p. 69 and V Kartov, ibid. p. 448.

wretched refugees, packed them together like sardines and callously relocated them by colonising Macedonia so as to provide cannon fodder for future wars.

Like the Bulgarian and Serbian bourgeoisie, the Greek bourgeoisie terrorises sections of the Thracian and Macedonian people and their lands with fire and sword. Without pressure on Macedonia, Thrace or other peoples, the bourgeoisie cannot be supported by us to restore social rights. Our bourgeoisie are the exploiters and oppressors of the Macedonians and the Thracians as well as exploiters and oppressors of the working class and poverty stricken peasants and refugees. If we do not destroy the control of the bourgeoisie over Macedonia and Thrace, we will not be able to break the social yoke under which that same bourgeoisie holds us all captive. There is no escape from the imperialist war about to be unleashed on us while the present situation of divide and rule by the Balkan and Turkish bourgeoisie is maintained.

This is why we struggle against weapons, against war which capitalism is preparing to unleash, against the oppression of the people and their forced exploitation. This is why we struggle for the union of the three parts of Macedonia and Thrace and for their national independence. This is why we demand national committees (Soviets) for refugees and peasants in a free and independent Macedonia so that we ourselves may share out the land among poor emigre farmers in accordance with their own interests. Only then will we save the exhausted refugees in Macedonia".[132]

For the first time in the "*Resolution*", mention is made of the Macedonian people and thus a de facto recognition of their existence. It refers to the

[132] R Kirjazovski, ibid. p. 9.

inhuman exploitation and political aims of the Greek authorities in colonising the whole of Aegean Macedonia with refugees from Bulgaria, Turkey and the Caucasus in accordance with the peace treaties signed in Paris and Lausanne.

The "*Resolution*" of the III Extraordinary Congress was an attempt by the "*Majority*" fraction of the CPG to tackle the Macedonian question and find a solution. The views of the "*Minority*" fraction, however, at odds with the "*Majority*" were rejected and dismissed as "*Trotskyist*" and "*opportunistic*".[133] The Comintern's Balkan expert, Dmitriy Manuilskiy, said that" *Kordhatos represented Social-democratic views for he was himself the embodiment of Bavarian Austro-Socialism*".[134]

Immediately after the decisions of the III Extraordinary Congress of the CPG, the Party found itself in deep crisis because of the Comintern's decision about Macedonia. At the same time this crisis coincided with the stabilisation of the Greek economy. The Greek authorities had colonised Macedonia with an enormous number of Christian population Greek and Turkish-speakers from Bulgaria, Turkey and the Caucasus, all thanks to the financial aid given by the League of Nations. This same aid enabled Greece to achieve political stability which had been seriously threatened after its defeat at the hands of the Turks under genial Kemal Pasha at the Sakarya river, 24 August 1921.[135] This defeat dealt Greece a grievous blow firstly because Greek forces were within 50

---

133 Y Kordhatos, To ethiniko zitima kai i efthini tis epitropis Pouliopoulou, Rizospastis 17/2/1927 p. 3 in Kiselinovski, ibid. p. 69.

134 R Kirajzovski, ibid. p. 40.

135 B Lewis, Narodziny Nowoczesnej Turcji, Warszawa 1972, p. 303, also M Tanty, Bosfor i Dardanele w polityce Mocarstw, Warszawa 1982, p. 339, D. Kołodziejczyk, Turcja, Warszawa 2000, p.107and 109. In all these authors the dates of these events differ one day.

kilometres of Ankara and its fall would have automatically broken Turkish resistance and given Greece enormous territorial gains. Secondly, after the disaster of Sakarya, Greek forces in turn began to suffer heavy defeats. On 29 July 1921 after three days of fightings they lose the battle upon Dumlupinar[136] which automatically resulted in breaking the Greek defence line. The Turks seized Smyrna [Tur. Izmir] on 8 September 1922 which was occupied by the Greek forces from 15 May 1919 till 8 September 1922 and in which in the beginning of occupation the Greek Army committed the massacre of the Islamic population[137] and contributed to the Turkish liberation war led by Mustafa Kemal called later Ataturk (the father of all Turks).[138]

---

[136] D. Kołodziejczyk, Turcja, Warszawa 2000, p.109, http://en.wikipedia.org/wiki/Battle_of_Dumlupinar

[137] The Greek troops and the local Greeks who had joined them in arms started a general massacre of the Mussulmen population in which the officials and Ottoman officers and soldiers as well as the peaceful inhabitants were indiscriminately put to death and subjected to forms of torture and savagery worthy of the Inquisition and constituting in any case a barbarous violation of the laws of humanity. Naturally the outcry was great among the Mussulmen population. The whole nation rose to oppose the barbarously hostile action of the Greeks. Meetings were organized in the towns and even in the villages and telegrams dispatched by the hundred to the Entente Powers and the whole civilized world, tearfully appealing for protection and help. in: James Harbord, Conditions in the Near East: Report of the American Military Mission to Armenia Government Printing Office, Washington, 1920 pp. 30—31 see http://armenianhouse.org/harbord/conditions-near-east.htm

[138] http://en.wikipedia.org/wiki/Kemal_Ataturk, V. D. Volkan, On Kemal Ataturk's psychoanalytic biography, in Turkish Studies, Vol. 13, Nos.1&2, 2007, pp. 229–241.

Mustafa Kemal Pasha

Source: http://en.wikipedia.org/wiki/File:Chrysostomos_of_Smyrna.jpg[download: 30.11.2011].
Source: http://en.wikipedia.org/wiki/File:Sakalli_Nureddin_-_Mirliva.jpg[download: 30.11.2011].

After the capture of the city of Smyrna on 8 September 1922 in retaliation which led to the massacre of the Christian population – Greek and Armenian as well as to the burning of the city[139]. 30 000 people were

[139] http://en.wikipedia.org/wiki/Great_Fire_of_Smyrna

murdered. Among them the Archbishop of Smyrna Chrysostomos Kalafatis[140] knowned as the Saint Chrysostomos of Smyrna. He was linched on 9 September 1922 by the mob instigated by the commander in chief of the Turkish forces Nureddin Pasha[141]. His beard was teared apart, his eyes were gouged out and then his nose and ears were cut off. On 13 September 1922 it came to the burning of the city the so-called great fire of Smyrna.[142]

Source: http://en.wikipedia.org/wiki/File:Great_Fire_of_Smyrna.jpg [download: 30.11.2011].
Source: http://en.wikipedia.org/wiki/File:Asia_Minor_massacres.jpg [download: 30.11.2011].

The rest of the population of the city run for its life by escaping with boats reaching the Great Powers vessels which were mooring in the bay[143].

On 18 September 1922 Mustafa Kemal announced that the "*whole of Anatolia had been liberated from the Greek yoke*".[144] However according to the

---

[140] M.Gleny, os.cit. p. 390, R. Clogg, os. cit. p. 116, A. Mango, Ataturk, John Murray (Publishers) Ltd, London 2002, p. 345, http://en.wikipedia.org/wiki/Chrysostomos_of_Smyrna

[141] http://en.wikipedia.org/wiki/Nureddin_Pasha

[142] A. Mango, os. cit., pp. 345-346, S. Kiselinovski, Istorija na sovremena Grcija, p. 35, http://en.wikipedia.org/wiki/Great_Fire_of_Smyrna

[143] On military catastrophy of the Greek Army in Anatolia see M. L. Smith, The Ionian vision. Greece in Asia minor 1919-1922, C. Hurst & Co., London 2005, pp. 284-311.

[144] J. Reychman, os. cit. p. 303, T. Wituch, Tureckie przemiany, p. 268, B. Dancig, os. cit., p. 97 writes that „K 18 sientiabria połnostiu była oćiščiena ot griekov vsia Zapadnaja AnatolijaA. F. Miller, os. cit, „..gienieral'nyj štab Grecii v Afinach tol'ko 20 sientjabrja opublikował miełancholičeskoie soobščienie o tom, čto griečieskaja armija „zakončiła svoi opieracii v Małoj Azii", praktičieski s vychodom turieckich vojsk k Egiejskomu morju grieko-turieckaja vojna była zavieršiena".

agreement signed at Mudanya[145] on 11 October 1922, Greece had to withdraw its forces to behind the Maritsa river in Thrace[146]. The Peace Conference opened at Lausanne[147] on 20 November 1922 and on 24 July 1923 the final peace treaty was signed[148] which granted sovereignty to Turkey[149] and confirmed its frontiers as they were in 1915[150] — frontiers which remain to this day.[151]

Map 5. Turkey's borders after the Lausanne Conference

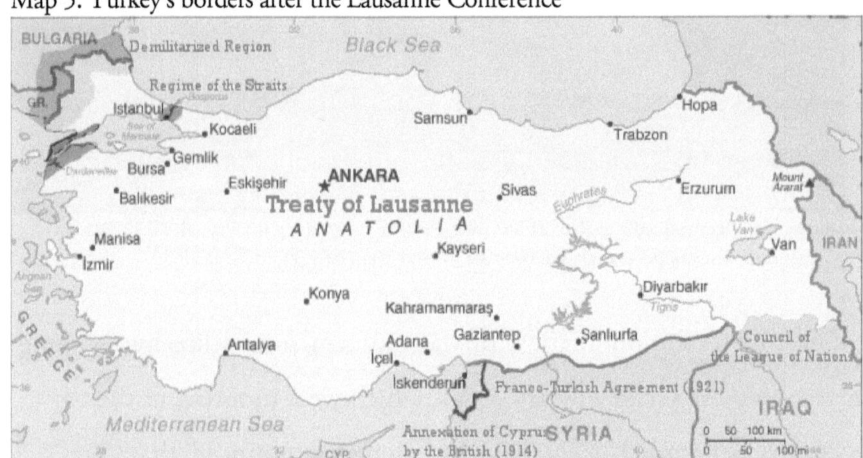

Source: http://en.wikipedia.org/wiki/File:Turkey-Greece-Bulgaria_on_Treaty_of_Lausanne.png [download: 30.11.2011].

---

[145] B. Dancig, os. cit, p. 98, B. Lewis, os. cit, p. 304, A. Baran Dural, os. cit, pp. 98–99, S. Kiselinovski, op.cit, p. 35, http://en.wikipedia.org/wiki/Armistice_of_Mudanya.

[146] B. Dancig, Ibidem, p. 98

[147] H. Batowski, Państwa bałkańskie 1800-1923, Kraków 1938, p. 273, B. Dancig, Ibidem, p. 99, A. Baran Dural, Ibidem, pp. 103 –106, E J. Zurcher, Turcja. Od sułtanatu do współczesności, Wyd. UJ, pp. 160–162.

[148] B. Lewis, Ibidem, p. 304 a treaty text see in The foundation of the Modern Greek state. Major treaties and conventions (1830–1947) (ed. Photini Constantopoulou), Kastaniotis Editions, Athens 1999, pp. 123–145, http://pl.wikipedia.org/wiki/Traktat_w_Lozannie, http://en.wikipedia.org/wiki/Treaty_of_Lausanne.

[149] T. Wituch, ibid. p. 268.

[150] H. Batowski, ibid. p. 273.

[151] T. Wituch, ibid., p. 268.

After these turbulent events, a period of calm ensued during which the Communist movement in Greece stagnated. However, friction between the *Majority* and *Minority* factions in the Party did not diminish but, on the contrary, increased as a result of the adoption of the policy of a united and independent Macedonia. This friction was in fact the sign of a deeper crisis in the Party itself which concerned the interpretation of Marxism as it applied to Greek society and to Greek historical awareness.[152] The *Minority* demanded that the broad tenets of Marxism be adapted to Greek society as it was whereas the *Majority* supported the wholesale adoption of Marxism as an infallible dogma to Greek society without reference to its specific identity. This was in contradiction to Greek mentality.

In 1925 Yanis Kordhatos elucidated the idealogical stance of the Minority in the pages of *Rizospastis*.

"The Party cannot ignore its historical past and exist outside the present. As every communist knows, Bolshevism means the adaptation of the general principles of Leninism to the actual conditions prevailing in any given country ... Communists have to demonstrate sufficient intelligence to understand the actual political and social problems of their own country bearing in mind that one single situation cannot obtain for all countries but quite the contrary, different situations arise according to different political and economic conditions. Crises in the Party and stagnation in the working class movement cannot be solved by personal attacks

[152] S. Kiselinovski, ibid. p. 72.

or dogmatic utterances. The fundamental tenets of Marxism must be adapted to Greek historical reality which we must endeavour to analyse objectively."[153]

A similar approach was adopted by H Vatis in his article "*Further to the Discussion about the Self-styled Protectors*" (Rizospastis 24 February 1927) His view was that "*Marxism and Leninism are inseparable from the revolutionary struggle and that they would be devalued if they were regarded as dogma or Holy Writ*".[154]

An interesting situation arose in the Party in 1926. Pantelis Pouliopoulos, First Secretary of the CPG and leader of the Majority faction since 1924 accepted the political views of the Minority. He wrote;

"the main reason for the stagnation in the Greek working class movement and the Communist cause in Greece is that there are no attempts in the Party to assimilate and transform Marxism-Leninism and make it relevant to the social and economic conditions prevailing in our country".[155]

Pouliopoulos went on to say that:

"in order to overcome the stagnation of the Greek working class movement, we first have to acquaint ourselves more thoroughly with the concrete problems which confronts the Party each day then to examine Greek historical reality in the light of Marxist doctrines".[156]

---

153 Y Kordhatos, Iperano olon to Koma kai oli ta prosopa, alla miliktos aghonas kata tis iperaristeras, "Rizospastis" 21/2/1927 in Kiselinovski, ibid. p. 71.

154 Vatis, Ligha ghia tin sizitisi...."Rizospastis" 24/2/1927 in Kiselinovski, ibid. p. 72.

155 P Pouliopoulos, Me pia enia mporoume na milisoume ghia istorikes "diomorfies" tu kinimatos mas, "Rizospastis" 6/2/1927 in Kiselinovski, ibid. p. 72.

156 P Pouliopoulos, Ghia to melon tou Komatos. "Rizospastis" 7/12/1927 in Kiselinovski, ibid. p. 72.

He concluded that:

"only in this way can the Party describe Greek objective reality according to Marxists tenets. Without adapting Marxism to Greek reality, the working class movement in Greece will not emerge from the grave crisis in which it has found itself since 1923".[157]

The Minority, attached to its pure ideological interpretation, attacked the aim of a united and independent Macedonia and at the same time demanded that the policy be abandoned. The Minority thought that after the migration of people from Turkey, Bulgaria and the Caucasus to Greece and from Greece to Turkey, a new ethnic — historical reality had emerged in Aegean Macedonia in which the Greeks were now in the majority. The result was that for the Minority, the aim of a united and independent Macedonia contradicted the new reality. A letter written by Alkidhamos (pseudonym for Yanis Kordhatos) published in the *Revolution Proletarienne* of 20 August 1926 stated that "*all the inhabitants of Greek Macedonia are Greeks because the Greek bourgeoisie has expelled the Slav population and settled Greek Macedonia with Greek refugees*".[158] Pouliopoulos, accepting the arguments of Kordhatos about adapting pure ideology to Greek realities and recalling the 1924 crisis of the Party, wrote in 1927;

"The problem of Macedonia will not go away and keeps recurring in one form or another, demanding of each political party a clear statement of policy. For the CPG the dilemma is acute; either to continue to support the aim of a United and Independent Macedonia or to reject it. This policy (I refer to the mistaken policy of

---

157 P Pouliopoulos, Me pia enia.."Rizospastis" 6/2/1927 in Kiselinovski, ibid. p. 72.

158 Letter by Alkidhamos (Y Kordhatos) published in "Revolution Proletarienne" in Kiselinovski ibid. p. 73.

defending the rights of all oppressed peoples to self-determination and separate development if they so wish) aiming at a United and Independent Macedonia and a United and Independent Thrace, rejected by the CPG and somehow explained away as our stance towards the problem of nationalities, is bankrupt and cannot be anything but bankrupt because it is a reflection not only of a mistaken assessment of the balance of forces in the country but also of revolutionary romanticism. The policy ignores the concrete realities of the revolutionary movement in the country, especially in Greek Macedonia and Thrace which any policy towards the national minorities has to take into account. It ignores both the absence of any popular-revolutionary forces in Greece and the enormous changes brought about by the influx of refugees and the danger for the CPG if the rank and file neither understand nor accept it..."[159]

We note here how the attitudes of the CPG, even amongst the representatives of the Majority have begun to move in the direction of the Minority. Poliopolous consistently failed to appreciate the distinctive nature of the Macedonian nation and he viewed it purely in geographical rather than in national terms and failed to notice any revolutionary currents there. Indeed he could not have noticed them for what he actually saw were Greek refugees from Bulgaria, Turkey and the Caucasus who did not demand separation from Greece. Nevertheless the aspirations of the Macedonians were precisely that. The enthusiasm with which the Macedonians embraced the Communist movement was extinguished because when speaking of a Macedonian nation, the Party leadership had in mind a Macedonian minority living on

[159] R Kirjazovski, ibid. pp. 28–29.

Macedonian territory yet were unable to discern a Macedonian people. This way of "*looking but not seeing*" was shared by Kordhatos who precipitated a crisis in the Party by referring to romanticism and immaturity in the revolutionary movement of the minority living in Macedonia. This is what he wrote about the mistaken policy of the Party concerning a *United and Independent Macedonia* in *Rizospastis*, 8 February 1927:

"Speakers on political matters at the Congress [the reference is to the crucially important congress of the CPG in 1924] presented Greek and Balkan realities with naive romanticism, describing them not as they actually were but as they wanted them to be. The Party, influenced by the youthful naiveté of its new leadership, thought it could act decisively on Balkan affairs. Such certainty made the leadership think that the prospect (of autonomy) was imminent and so they devoted all their efforts to settling the problem of the nationalities. These efforts were in vain because the minorities did not respond [in the revolutionary sense] and the working class showed not the slightest interest. Moreover, these efforts demonstrated that the Party leadership, buoyed up by enthusiasm, turned the Party overnight into a party of national minorities."[160]

As a result of this article, the controversy surrounding the problems of the nationalities not only became more acute, but provoked fresh reactions from the members of the CPG. The question was raised whether in fact the Macedonian question really was central to the affairs of the CPG or merely peripheral.[161] An answer was provided by Gheorghios Siantos in an article in *Rizospastis* of 13 March 1927:

---

[160] Ibid. p. 32.

[161] S Kiselinovski, ibid. pp. 76–77.

> "Up to now no comrade has explained the problem of the nationalities clearly enough for all members of the Party to understand. The issue of the national minorities is either of fundamental or strategic concern of the CPG. How we handle this issue is a measure of whether we govern well or badly. This issue was raised during the 1924 Congress and the reasons for our failure lay in our tactical and organisational shortcomings. However, in my view, the issue of the national minorities can never be fundamental to the CPG. The fundamental issue of the CPG is the class struggle aimed at the overthrow of Capitalism and the establishment of Communism. Therefore any other movement which weakens capitalism can be supported and even fought for but only in so far as it contributes to achieving the final aim. In this sense, I consider that our policy towards the problem of the nationalities has been mistaken from the very beginning. Despite the fact that we have different views, I do not think that the crisis in the Party had anything to do with this policy. The Party should formulate its policy concerning the national minorities with the ultimate aim in sight."[162]

Siantos thus considers that the main problem cannot be in principle the nationality question but the class struggle. The previous policy of a *United and Independent Macedonia* is described as "*mistaken from the very beginning*". This statement recalls that of another Greek communist, Vatis, who expressed his opinion in the 24 March 1927 edition of *Rizospastis* as follows;

[162] R Kirjazovski, ibid. p. 66.

THE NATIONAL QUESTION AND OUR PARTY

I. Is it a principal or strategic problem? Let us start to raise a theoretical question.

"Discussion from 1924 (besides the theory on "maturity") which was led (in question) whether the problem of the national minorities is a fundamental or a strategic issue with reference to Siantos' article. Concerning the former, we should consider the various stages in the struggles of the proletariat. One of these is the overthrow of imperialism. The victory over imperialism is impossible without the liberation of the colonies which provide the imperialists with such powerful economic support and this means that the struggle to liberate oppressed peoples is a "fundamental" issue for the Party. No Communist Party can exist without recognising the inevitability of such struggles with all their practical consequences, otherwise it would be a Social-Democratic Party. Therefore the nationality problem is at the same time a "strategic" one. The final strategic aim is the overthrow of imperialism and in this struggle we are obliged to make use of all revolutionary means which also include the national liberation of oppressed peoples. We must therefore consider Macedonia a "fundamental" issue if we recognise its right to self-determination and separation but as a "strategic" one if we fight for a united proletarian front to liberate oppressed peoples".[163]

For Vatis, though not for Siantos, the "*struggle to liberate oppressed peoples*" is a "*fundamental*" issue for the Party. But the nationality problem, he declares, is at the same time a strategic issue, for the aim is the "*overthrow of imperialism and in this struggle we are obliged to use all revolutionary means including liberation movements*".

[163] ibid. pp. 69–70.

So the CPG Congress of 1924 which adopted the aim of a *United and Independent Macedonia* became the scene of endless disputes concerning whether adopting this aim was a mistake or not. The reason for this was the lack of anything which might distinguish the Macedonians from others living in Macedonia. This was in turn the reason why Macedonians became noticeably cooler towards the CPG, precipitating an internal crisis, the true nature of which was not understood by the members of the CPG. The Third Extraordinary Congress of the CPG was held in a stormy and crisis-laden atmosphere during which the slogan "*A United and Independent Macedonia*" was defended — a clear sign of the gradual recognition of the Macedonian question by CPG members. This Third Congress took place in Athens on 6 April 1927. The CPG *Resolution* at this Congress reads as follows:

III Congress of the CPG

From statement on executive committees work

From the Extraordinary Congress, November 1924,

From Third Ordinary Congress

THE NATIONAL MINORITIES QUESTION

"The Extraordinary Congress of 1924 defined the Party's policy towards the question of the national minorities. Because the Party erred in its handling of this issue and because some comrades attempted to force changes in the decisions of the Congress, the Party has decided the following:

1 The views of the comrades who proposed to reject the slogan of a "United and Independent Macedonia" are mistaken for they rest on dubious arguments about the ex-

istence and status of the Macedonian and Thracian people. The starting point for any Bolshevik definition of any particular case is the question, to what extent in any given country is there evidence of an oppressed minority and how can this minority be mobilised, together with the working class, to fight the ruling bourgeoisie who oppress it?

2 The principles of national self-determination and freedom from oppression should be enshrined in Party policies towards the question of national minorities. During 1923/4 when a revolutionary situation existed in the Balkans, the Balkan Communist Federation and the Comintern proposed an "Independent Macedonia" to define our basic policy towards the national minorities and at the same time to harness the revolutionary masses living in Thrace and Macedonia, which were divided up among four countries, for the struggle against the Pan-Balkan bourgeoisie. The best weapon in our struggle against the imperialist tendencies of Serbia and Bulgaria was the slogan "A United Macedonia and Thrace".

3 Although we are not at present in a revolutionary phase, the aim of a "United and Independent Macedonia" should remain. The path from the revolutionary phase to serious preparations influences the Party line on national minority matters as we explain below. The CPG is currently committed to put forward the first plan which does not involve a struggle to realise the above aim but rather concerns itself with concrete measures to remove the means of national oppression (taxes, agricultural policies, language, colonisation etc.) The struggle must continue by means of the press and Party activity both inside and outside parliament. Besides this, the Party is committed to promote the aim of a "United and Independent Macedonia" which brings with it the immediate danger of a new Balkan war and at the same time to promote the aim of a Federal Republic of Balkan Workers and Farmers in which it will become possible to settle national minority issues. The Party is also committed to acquainting itself with the ways national minorities are oppressed in Greece and take effective measures to deal with them.

4 The Party's mistake at the 1924 Congress was that it placed the question of the national minorities at the centre of its activities. From 1925 the Party's error did not lie in the slogan as such but rather in the place assigned to it among other slogans and activities of the Party.

5 Downplaying the slogan "Independent Macedonia" during the last parliamentary elections was a mistake.

6 The Congress stressed the need to step up internationalist propaganda among the toiling masses and intensify the struggle against the bourgeoisie's nationalist and chauvinistic propaganda, especially amongst immigrant populations.Ideological training is necessary to counter new wars and to strengthen worker resistance to the oppression of the national minorities. "[164]

The "*Resolution*" itself was confirmed by the decision taken earlier at the 1924 Congress. The confirmation of the slogan "*United Macedonia*" was the response of the CPG to those members who wished to reject it. There was open acknowledgement of the Party's mistakes such as those concerning the national minorities and the absence of the slogan "*Independent Macedonia*" during the elections. Attention was drawn to the increased internationalist propaganda among the toiling masses and the necessity to counter the effects of nationalistic and chauvinistic propaganda. Paragraph 1 of the Resolution pointed out that rejection of the slogan "*United and Independent Macedonia and Thrace*" was mistaken as it was based on dubious arguments. The Congress pushed through changes in its Macedonian policy; by accepting the slogan "*United and Independent Macedonia*" it hoped to overcome the crisis which had arisen in 1924. A thorough analysis of this crisis including the reasons for the non-participation of Macedonians in the Greek Communist

[164] ibid. pp. 76–78. The document says about Philip Draghoumis who belonged to the Tsaldaris party. He was a governor of Aegean (Greek) Macedonia with its seat in Salonika. What regards Gheorghios Modhis he belonged to the Tsaldaris party and he was a governor of Epirus with its seat in Ioannina. He was Valahian and knew Macedonian well because he lived in Florina (Lerin) which was populated by Macedonians and still is to this day. I received this information from Professor Simiczijew who lived in those times in Greece and was good observer of these events.

movement was given by Nikos Kyriakopoulos in his article "*Why the Macedonians spurn the United Front - A response to Messrs Dhraghoumis and Modhis*"[165] which appeared in *Rizospastis* on 8 April 1927.

Map 6. The Florina Prefecture

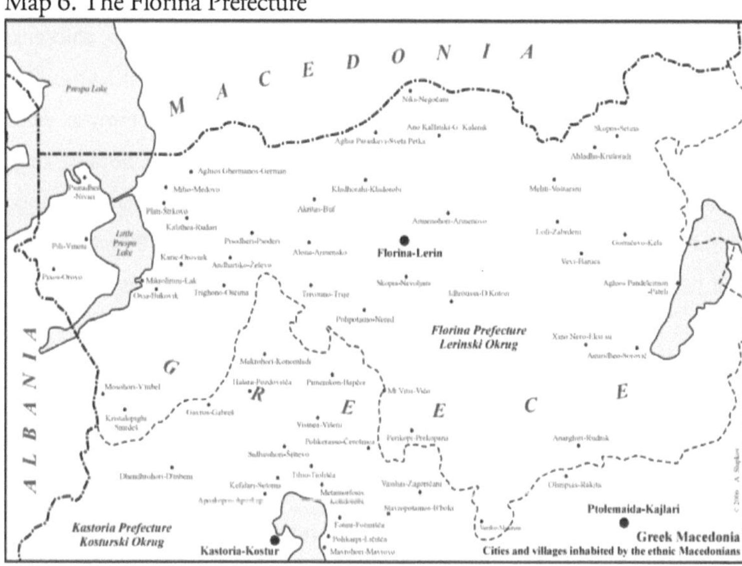

Map by the author.

"We are duty bound to reply to Messrs Dhraghoumis and Modhis's attack, not against the Communists but against the rural population in Macedonia and against Macedonia in general. The Macedonians consider themselves to be a proud people who were among the first to understand their place in modern society, probably because they suffered very badly from capitalist exploitation and from those who wielded power in their lands as well as from the imperial superpowers who hold the Balkans in thrall. The imperialist forces subjected the Macedonians to appalling treatment during the war. Serbia and Eastern Macedonia were totally devastated by the Bulgarians and by "civilised" defenders of the people. All young men were rounded up and 90% of them died in Bulgaria at the hands of Bulgarian thugs. Most of the villages were razed to the ground. Whole

165 "United Front" founded by the CPG, the Greek Farmers Party and other progressive organisations. Editorial note in the documents, p. 78.

families were deported and the majority of young girls raped by "cultured" Frenchmen and Englishmen. Women from the villages around lake Ohrid/Prespa[166] German, [Grk. Aghios Germanos,] Medovo, [Grk. Milio], Štrkovo, [Grk. Plati], Rudari, [Grk Kalithea], Orovnik, [Grk. Karie], Lak, [Grk. Mikrolimni] and many others were forced to leave them without taking anything with them and when they returned they found only heaps of rubble. The Macedonians have learnt to make the most of what they have to satisfy their needs. To feed his family, every farmer must have sheep, two or three oxen, chickens, pigs, granaries and sufficient equipment to cultivate his smallholding of 2 or 3 acres. Oxen from these villages and most of the sheep were requisitioned by the army as were their horse-drawn carts, horses and pigs and many villagers were beaten because they tried to conceal something in order to survive. Those whom the Bulgarians accused of being sympathetic to the Greeks are now accused by the Greeks of being Bulgarians and supporters of the Komits [small groups of partisans fighting against Turkish rule, later Greek rule].

Understandably the Macedonians learnt bitter lessons from these experiences before eventually finding their role in the class struggle and seeking allies. Everybody who took up their cause betrayed them and turned against them. They have no confidence in the United Front of Workers and Peasants because they do not know any candidates nor are they interested in the tactics of the Party. I can assure you, Messrs Draghoumis and Modhis that the Lerin constituency[167] did not vote for Kyriakopoulos but for the United Front of Workers and Peasants and Refugees. It is an utter lie to say that I deceived the voters. They knowingly voted for the hammer and sickle. "[168]

---

[166] Villages around Lake Prespa. The lake is divided between the present-day republics of Albania, Greece and Macedonia.

[167] The town of Lerin in Aegean Macedonia, mainly inhabited by Macedonians. After the names were changed from Macedonian to Greek in 1919, it became known as Florina. On this change of names; see What Europe Has Forgotten: The Struggle of the Aegean Macedonians, Politecon Publications, Sydney 1993. Also L Mojsov, Okolu prašanjeto na makedonskoto nacionalno malcinstvo vo Grcija, Skopje 1954, T. H. Simovski, Atlas of the inhabited places of Aegean Macedonia. Skopje 1997, C. Stefou, History of the Macedonia people from ancient times to the present. Toronto 2005.

[168] R Kirjazovski, ibid. pp. 78–79.

The views of Nikos Kyriakopoulos, a representative of the United Front differ considerably from those of many predecessors in the depth of his analysis and his understanding of the Macedonian problem. This may be because he was of Vlach origin [a pastoral people originally from Romania who emigrated to Macedonia][169] and lived in Psoderi (Gr. Pisodheri) in the Lerin district of Macedonia. His article demonstrates for the first time the difficult situation of the Macedonians from his own perspective.

Pisodheri / Psoderi at present. Photo by the author.

His statement that the Macedonians "*found their role in the class struggle and sought allies*" is the best proof for Kyriakopoulos of their receptiveness to the CPG for it was not him they voted for but for the "*hammer and sickle*". This article marks a change in the CPG's attitude towards the Macedonian

[169] J Czekanowski, Wstęp do Historji Słowian, Lwów 1927, pp. 74–77.

national problem At times he was a lone voice among many others who saw the problem quite differently. By contrast, consider the views expressed in the "*Resolution*" of the Third Plenum of the CPG Central Committee of 27-31 January 1930.

" *The issue of the national minorities does not play a large part in Greece because of the relatively small numbers of oppressed people. The strength of the revolutionary movement in Greece is the proletariat, the bulwark of the revolution together with its allies - active groups in the towns fighting national and foreign capitalists and imperialists and resolutely opposed to the relics of feudalism, poor farmers, the petty bourgeoisie, the oppressed peasantry and small-time urban landlords".*[170]

The "*Resolution*" generally ignores the existence of national minorities in Greece. It concentrates on the strength of the proletariat, the "*bulwark of therevolution*". The CPG's lack of any engagement with the issue of Macedonia provoked severe criticism from the Comintern in 1931.[171] In March of that year it criticised the CPG for:

> "... contenting itself with merely emphasising the slogan "United and Independent Macedonia" without attempting to bring it about by a national struggle for self-determination within the overall struggle of the working class"[172]

Shortly after this criticism, in June 1931, the presidium of the Comintern organised a conference devoted to the question of the national minorities in capitalist Europe. During the conference, Otto Kuusinen sharply criticised the

---

170 R Kirjazovski, ibid. p. 90.

171 V Kartov, os. cit. p. 451.

172 http://pl.wikipedia.org/wiki/Otto_Kuusinen, http://en.wikipedia.org/wiki/Otto_Kuusinen

communist parties of the Balkans for their handling of the national minorities on the grounds that they treated them like pure abstractions.

> "With these attitudes they obstructed their members' struggles against concrete forms of national oppression, for freedom to secede and for national liberation from the subjugation of the Balkan bourgeoisie."[173]

However, in November 1931 the Comintern intervened in the affairs of the CPG. It published an open letter listing all the errors the CPG had committed over the national minority issue. The letter stated:

> "... the CPG has distanced itself from the revolutionary struggles of the oppressed peoples in Greece. It makes no effort to take part in their struggles or take advantage of the enormous goodwill which the Communists enjoy among the oppressed peoples such as the Macedonians, Turks, Albanians, Jews... The CPG does not react as it should to anti-Semitism and to the subjugation of Macedonians and Turks, nor does it reveal the background of the policies of the Greek bourgeoisie. It is the duty of the Party to prosecute without delay the struggle against the national oppression and persecution of the Macedonians and to enforce their rights to self-determination and separate development."[174]

The second stage in the history of the CPG is thus concluded during which the establishment of an independent Macedonia was mentioned but not one word about the Macedonians themselves living there. Where they are mentioned, they are lumped together with all the other nationalities living in Macedonia without any indication that they have lived there for centuries.

---

[173] Otto Kuusinen, O Natsionalnom Voprosie v kapitalističeskoi Yevropie, Kommunističeski Internatsional, No. 23/1931 in V Kartov ibid. p. 452.

[174] Sarnada hronia aghones to KKE 1918–1958 in V Kartov, ibid. pp. 452–453.

Only in 1930 does the CPG finally begin to change its attitude towards the Macedonian national problem. This will be the subject of my next chapter.

CHAPTER

4

THE CPG AND ITS POLICY OF "NATIONHOOD WITHOUT STATEHOOD" 1935-40

After strong pressure and an appeal from the Comintern, the CPG was forced to adopt a position towards the Macedonian issue. A clear sign of change in the CPG was its acknowledgement of the Comintern's intervention and the appointment of a new Central Committee in 1930, consisting of Nikos Zahariadhis, Yanis Ioanidhis, Stilianos Sklavenas, Yanis Mihalidhis, Vasilis Nefeloudhis, Leonidhas Stringhos and G Konstandinidhis.[175] In the words of the Macedonian historian, Stojan Kiselinovski, a noted authority on the history of the CPG and its relations with Macedonia,

> *"the formation of a new Central Committee in 1931 marks the end of the 'prehistoric' epoch in the CPG's history and the beginning of the 'historic' period. The CPG began to demonstrate greater political realism and formulate policies in accordance with Greek historical reality but without entirely escaping political dogmatism which was to remain an abiding feature of its policies during the whole period".*[176]

175 S Kiselinovski, Egejskiot del na Makedonija (1913–1989) Skopje 1990, p. 89.

176 ibid. pp. 89–90.

It was an unusually accurate assessment. The Party's denial of the very existence of a Macedonian problem, which was patently obvious to CPG members but ignored for ideological reasons, can only be called "*prehistoric*" because it ignored historical reality. Once the problem had been recognised and an attempt made to resolve it, then it could be said that from 1931 the CPG had indeed entered a "*historic*" phase. Articles began to appear in the official journal of the CPG, "*Rizospastis*", about the Macedonians living in Aegean Macedonia and their sad fate. The first article marking the CPG's new approach was entitled "*How a certain weary nation was forcibly hellenised by Greek Andarts and Bulgarian Komits*"[177] and appeared in "*Rizospastis*" under the sub-title "*With Macedonians in Macedonia*".

> "Macedonia, November. It is an indisputable fact that up to now very little has been written about the lives and circumstances of the Macedonian people. Today the matter has taken on a new meaning for us and our cause for our presence among them is now essential. Let us give a short outline of the problem based on adequate documentation. There is no doubt that in the Balkans no other people has been so badly treated as the Macedonians. They have been continuously oppressed for over 500 years. First they were under the lash of the Turks, then the Greeks and Bulgarians. When the Bulgarian, Serbian and Greek bourgeoisie intervened to take them under their "protection", the Macedonians began to be brutally persecuted. Gangs of Andarts and Komits in a series of acts unprecedented in Macedonian history burned their villages and murdered their inhabitants. Macedonians will never forget the bestial acts of Captains Lakis and Vardhas [Nikola Dailakis, an Andarts leader was killed by partisans in 1941 for collaboration with the enemy during the wartime occupation of Greece; Kontos Vardhas was also an Andarti leader — see footnote for further details]. Whole villages were drowned in blood which flowed in torrents. During the Balkan wars, the bourgeoisie of Greece, Bulgaria and Ser-

177 Komits – small bands of partisans numbering 15 to 20 fighting firstly against Turks and then against Macedonians to force them to support annexation to Bulgaria.

bia vied with each other in their attempts to oppress, seize and destroy Macedonians and their property. All this in the name of the "Party" for the "liberation of oppressed brothers" against the Macedonians who are neither Bulgarian, nor Greek nor Serb but just Macedonians. Those Macedonians who survived the [first] world war and Balkan wars returned home to their villages to rebuild their homes. But their sufferings were not over. Bulgarian Komits, faithful agents of the Bulgarian bourgeoisie continued their oppressive activities as did the fascists of the EEE [Union of the Greek People], faithful agents of the Greek bourgeoisie to add to the anguish of the Macedonians. The Greek, Bulgarian and Serbian bourgeoisie, each separately, have tried to seize and subjugate the Macedonian nation. Mention has been made mistakenly of the Bulgarian minority in capitalist Greece and the Greek minority in capitalist Bulgaria. This is a mistake. In Macedonia under Bulgarian, Greek or Serbian rule there are neither Greeks, Bulgarians nor Serbs — only Macedonians (apart from those who settled there recently). You only have to take a walk in the fields and mountains of Kostur [Gr. Kastoria] and Lerin [Gr. Florina] to be convinced of this. The answers they give us are in accordance with their nature and customs which bear no resemblance to those of the Greeks, Bulgarians or Serbs.

Undoubtedly, many years of oppression by the bourgeoisie have left their mark on the Macedonians but they are still distinguishable by their dress. They also have something very special, their language. This is a Slavonic language similar, but not the same as Bulgarian, although anybody knowing Macedonian can communicate with a Serb or a Bulgar. Today some one hundred thousand people[178] speak Macedonian as their native language, not knowing any other. The Slav tribes settled in Macedonia many centuries ago and today they know only that here they were born and here they will die. It is a fact that in many aspects of their treatment of Macedonia, the three capitalist powers have achieved a certain degree of success by means of fire and sword and depriving them of their national consciousness. The majority of the Macedonians now live in Western Macedonia around Lerin [Gr. Florina], Voden [Gr. Edhessa], Ber [Gr. Veria] and Kostur [Gr. Kastoria]. The attentive visitor will find whole villages in this area where sometimes Bulgarian and sometimes Greek is spoken. This is not unusual for they are their native languages

178 S Kiselinovski, Egejskiot del na Makedonija. Comparing the translations of this extract of the document, I opted for Kiselinovski's version which is much more precise and gives a more accurate number of people speaking Macedonian. See Egejskiot del na Makedonija (1913–89), Skopje 1990, p. 91.

because, as I have already said, this is the result of oppression and persecution by the Bulgarian bourgeoisie on numerous occasions.

B

Let us examine the facts. What are the living conditions of the Macedonian minority? In all respects, very poor. I will not mention economic pressures which are already known and are worse than in any other area. But some observations on their spiritual and political persecution would be in order so that working people in Greece may have some idea of the misery of the unfortunate Macedonians. Let us begin with their schools. Children are forced to learn Greek at school and are forbidden to speak Macedonian. If a child disobeys, he is detained by the teacher in a room for up to twenty four hours. If a policeman hears a child speaking Macedonian on the street, he will beat him. The same happens with adults. A case in point occurred in the village of Nestram [Gr. Nestorio] in the Kostur [Gr. Kastoria] district. The chief of police threatened to beat a teacher because he had spoken to a farmer in Macedonian. A school inspector in the same area kept secret files and demanded strict precautions to be taken especially with regard to those pupils whose fathers entertained ideas of national liberation.

IN LERIN

This oppression reached its culmination in the villages around Lerin and Korešta. Every day school children were interrogated to establish whether their parents had any contact with armed men, what language they spoke etc. At home they were all forced to speak Greek as part of the deliberate process of hellenisation. It is worth noting that none of their women can speak the language. The regional commander, Balkos, one of the most ruthless oppressors, was a leader of the Andarts and would constantly summon teachers to find out what was happening in the villages and would instruct them in the "national task" of oppressing Macedonians. There is of course not sufficient space in "Rizospastis" to give details of the many other facts. I will confine myself to saying that when previously Macedonia, under Greek rule was "governed" by bandits, Andarts and Komits, peasants were forced to change their views every day in order to save their lives. To the Komits they admitted they were Bulgars, to the Andarts they confessed they were

Greeks. Today they are forced to declare at every opportunity that they feel authentically Greek, otherwise they are exposed to the lash of the ever-present whis.

PRESSURE FROM THE RICH

Evil never rests. The whips of the Greek bourgeoisie served the interests of rich Macedonians. It was not sufficient to swear an oath of loyalty to Greece; it had to be "confirmed" by a rich Macedonian. Both collaborated in open plunder as in the days of the Andarts - rape, threats, confiscation. It was not enough to pay taxes to the state and community and, if the combination of the Andarts, exploitation of labour and political and spiritual repression was not enough, the rich joined in for their share as well.

I got to know an old peasant from , Gorničevo [Kela] who told me a typical story. One of his neighbours, who is now a merchant in Sorovič [Amindheo] borrowed sixty pounds from him to "confirm" to the local police that he was a Greek. This "Greek patriot" was also a Komit informer. Even his brother forsook the Komits leader Tanev. Rich Macedonians in his village were police informers for the Greeks just as in other villages they were police informers for the Bulgarians. They changed their nationality like the shirts on their backs, depending on who paid more. Only the industrious Macedonian people despite poverty and devastating persecution remained true to their nationality.

REPTILES FROM EEE (ETHNIKI ENOSIS ELLAS)

For poor Macedonians, the most terrifying persecutors were those who had once been andarti but were now leaders of the EEE [Union of Greek People] with Pavlos Melas [leader of the Andarts group renowned for its cruelty and ruthlessness in the fight against civilian Macedonians in Aegean Macedonia].[179] It is no exaggeration to say that the Andarts terrorised the Macedonians more than the police did. Last year, for example, in the centre of the market square in Lerin, a captain of the EEE, Vanghelis, thrashed a boy for speaking Macedonian while the police merely looked on. In V'mbel, Kostur district, [Gr. Kastoria], ten young men were beaten to a bloody pulp and then imprisoned

[179] See further in R Poplazarov, Grčkata politika sprema Makedonija vo vtorata polovina na XIX i početot na XX vek, Skopje 1973.

just because they sang songs in their native tongue. The same happened in the village of Aposkep [Gr. Aposkepos] to some boys who celebrated May Day by singing songs of liberation which had been translated into Macedonian. Going for a walk after nine o'clock was prohibited where the police were in evidence but there was no limit to the beatings and punishments incurred for breaking this prohibition. And what can we say about the terror visited on the land after the killing of a nationalist spy, Cantevski? No words can describe it. Whips and batons rained down on the bodies of hundreds of suspected Macedonians before the ringleaders, Manov, Peckov and Balaska were finally captured and shot, one after the other. The ordinary Macedonian looked on and trembled with fear; might not even the walls betray him if he said something in Macedonian?

MACEDONIA UNDER SERB AND BULGARIAN RULE

Not only Macedonians living under Greek bourgeois rule were persecuted but also those living in areas under Bulgarian and Serb rule. The Bulgarian authorities, the so-called *"National Coalition"* together with the Agrarian Fascist Party and the VMRO Komit organisation [a section of the VMRO collaborating with the Bulgarians who wanted to force Macedonians to work for the government] maltreated and abused ordinary Macedonians. Examples abound. In the area of Petrič and Nevrokop in Bulgaria [Bulg. Goce Delčev, a town in Pirin Macedonia] there is no freedom whatsoever. The Komits are totally in control and occupy positions in tobacco companies there. Every protest is instantly choked in blood. You can imagine how powerful the party is because over a period of nine years, two thousand Macedonians were killed out of a total population of over 180,000. Workers and peasants from other areas who were considered *"dangerous"* were sent to Petrič where groups of Komits under Mihailov considered them *"harmless"* and even killed them. Last month more than six hundred people left their homes and fields in Nevrokop and escaped to other areas to save themselves from Komits acting illegally.

The fascist officers of King Alexander of Serbia were equally as harsh. Under a fascist dictatorship 1500 Macedonians were killed, 3400 sentenced to various punishments and hard labour and thousands temporarily imprisoned. This is merely a pale outline of the appalling treatment meted out to the Macedonians, irrespective of whether their tor-

> mentors were members of the Greek, Bulgarian or Serbian bourgeoisie. One things is clear; they all tried to outdo each other in persecuting and exploiting the Macedonians. The capitalists did this as a matter of course but what can the Macedonians do to stop it?[180]

This was the first time the CPG concerned itself with the Macedonian issue at such length in the pages of "*Rizospastis*". The breakthrough was due to the recognition of Macedonian separate identity. I quote an excerpt from the above text;

In Macedonia under Bulgarian, Greek or Serbian rule there are neither Greeks, Bulgars nor Serbs – only Macedonians.

In this way the CPG expressed a definitive opinion about the actual presence of Macedonians living in Greece. This represents a complete change of policy for the CPG because previously they, the Macedonians, had been lumped together with Greeks, Serbs, Bulgars and Vlachs but now they acknowledged the distinct ethnic identity of Macedonians living in Aegean Macedonia. Moreover, the CPG referred in the article to their language, how it was *similar but not the same as Bulgarian and that it was spoken by 100,000 people.* This change of policy is the result of accepting reality in place of dogma. The article also describes the difficult situation of the Macedonians and for the first time depicts the severity and harshness of the ways in which they were hellenised. Mention is also made of the situation of Macedonians in Yugoslavia and Bulgaria.

[180] R Kirjazovski, KPG i makedonskoto nacionalno prašanje 1918–1974, Skopje 1982, pp. 96–101.

Another result of this change of policy was the acquiescence of the CPG to the formation of the Macedonian party, VMRO United, a continuation of the VMRO founded in 1893 in Salonika. The first meeting of the Macedonian revolutionaries took place at the bookshop of Ivan Hadži-Nikolov in Salonika on 28 October 1893. They were Dame Gruev, Hristo Tatarčev, Petar Pop-Arsov, Anton Dimitrov and Hristo Batandžiev.[181] Later they were joined by Goce Delčev,[182] one of the greatest of Macedonian heroes. The purpose of the meeting was to found a secret revolutionary organisation in order to prepare the Macedonian people for a national uprising and a declaration of independence. The result was the Ilinden Uprising[183] of 2 August 1903 which was brutally put down with heavy loss of life over a period of three months.[184] Despite this setback, the uprising demonstrated an increasingly more powerful sense of national consciousness amongst Macedonians. After the uprising, the great majority of the revolutionaries sought refuge in Bulgaria to escape the revenge of the Turks. Both before and after the Balkan wars, VMRO activities waned but started up again around 1925. In 1923/4, Vienna became the centre of more intense activity for Macedonian patriots escaping from Greece, Bulgaria and the Kingdom of the Serbs, Croats and Slovenes.[185] The CPB began discussions with all factions of Macedonians emigres in order to unite them and on 29 April 1924 Petar

---

181 Istorija na makedonskiot narod, Kniga vtora, Skopje 1969, p. 160.

182 See further in D Dimevski, Goce Delčev, Skopje 1992.

183 See further in M D Pandevski, Ilindenskoto vostanje vo Makedonija 1903, Skopje 1978.

184 J Skowronek, M Tanty, T Wasilewski, Historia Słowian południowych i zachodnich, Warszawa 1988, p. 510.

185 D Kartov, Makedonskiot narod i pravoto na samoopredeluvanje 1912-41, Skopje 1987, p. 241.

Čaulev[186] signed on behalf of the Central Committee of the VMRO a "*Declaration of the United Macedonian Revolutionary Movement*".[187] However, the most important document was the so-called "*May Manifesto*" which, in summary, stated that:

1 The Macedonian Revolutionary Movement must cooperate with the progressive and democratic forces of the Balkans and Europe.

2 War should be declared on the neighbouring states of Bulgaria, Greece and the KSCS because they oppose Macedonian self-determination.

3 The final aim is the liberation and unification of the divided parts of Macedonia into one completely independent and sovereign political entity within its own natural geographic and ethnic boundaries.[188]

The result of these resolutions was the founding in Vienna in October 1925 of the "*United InternalMacedonian RevolutionaryOrganisation*" known by its Macedonian initials as VMRO. At the inaugural congress, several programme documents were published including an "*Appeal to the Macedonian People and to World Public Opinion*", a Constitution and a "*Statement on the Situation of the Macedonian People*".[189] The *Statement* included an elaborate introduction and five sections. Below are the six aims and tasks which the VMRO undertook to achieve.

---

[186] Source: http://en.wikipedia.org/wiki/Petar_Chaulev, http://mk.wikipedia.org/wiki/ Петар_Чаулев, http://bg.wikipedia.org/wiki/ Петър_Чаулев, download 17.01.2015)

[187] ibid. p. 242.

[188] Majskiot manifest i deklaracijata na VMRO (Obedineta), Skopje, 1948, p 9–11 in D Kartov, os. cit. p. 243.

[189] D Kartov, os. cit. p. 245.

1 An increase in propaganda and agitation amongst the Macedonian people without distinction of nationality which would serve to organise the revolutionary struggle whose aim was to secure the liberation and unification of Macedonia as a political entity — an independent Republic of Macedonia and its federation with other free People's Republics in a Balkan Federation.

2 The continuation of the existing struggle and its integration with all other national and political organisations which promote the self-determination of nations and their membership in a federation of Balkan republics.

3 The unmasking of the political crimes of all Balkan powers, the struggle against their policy of divide and rule and of colonialisation and assimilation.

4 The unmasking of the imperialist policies of European countries towards Macedonia and the Balkans.

5 The waging of a merciless campaign against Macedonian traitors serving the interests of the Bulgarian, Greek and Serb imperialists.

6 The increase in propaganda and agitation abroad among the working class and progressive public opinion as well as among Macedonian and Balkan emigres for an independent Macedonia and a Balkan Federation.[190]

---

[190] Bulletin "Balkanskaya Federatsiya" no. 51/1.9.1926.

The fourth and fifth parts of the *Statement* assess the policies of Balkan states towards Macedonia:

1 Up to now the policies of the Balkan authorities have been clearly dictated by the imperialist interests of the bourgeoisie and the Balkan states.

2 The authorities are interested in Macedonia only in so far as they are able to extract maximum political capital for themselves and their dynasties from the sufferings of the Macedonian people.

3 The authorities are interested in Macedonia only in so far as they can carry out their imperialist policy of ruling it as a whole or divided up between them.

4 The authorities are opponents of Macedonian aspirations to liberty and unity.

5 All bourgeois political parties in the Balkans support and strengthen the policies of the authorities.

6 The only allies of the Macedonian people are other oppressed nations and the working classes of the Balkans. "[191]

From this introduction it is evident that the VMRO planned large-scale agitation activities amongst the Macedonians . It was emphasised that the existence of Macedonia would be the safest guarantee of a Balkan Federation, which, together with progressive political organisations, would be natural allies of the oppressed Macedonian people. The VMRO was well aware of the extent to which Macedonia was ruthlessly exploited by Greece, Bulgaria and the Kingdom of Serbs, Croats and Slovenes and by exposing this exploitation they

[191] ibid.

intended to win the support of the Macedonians. They very much counted on the support of the toiling masses who were also exploited by these countries. However, the fourth and fifth parts of the VMRO's *Statement* showed clearly the real motives of the rulers of the Balkan states bordering Macedonia — unbridled economic exploitation of Macedonia and its people resulting from its division. The strength which could help the aspirations of the Macedonians in their struggle for the creation of their own country was evident in the "*oppressed peoples and the working classes of the Balkans*".

All this demonstrated the unity of the VMRO and its intense patriotic character. In its own paper, *Makedonsko Delo*[192], it constantly emphasised the unity of the state and people. Writing on this subject, Pavel Šatev[193], a member of the VMRO noted;

> The Macedonian National Movement has expressed through its political representatives the demands of the Macedonians over many years for their own motherland, an independent Macedonian state with its own history and independent political life. Both the intelligentsia and the ranks of peasant farmers, skilled artisans and workers are one in this desire.[194]

It is of course entirely understandable that after Šatev's words about continuing the struggle for an independent Macedonian state, the activities of the VMRO were banned in all those countries which had occupied parts of Macedonia after the Peace Conference in Bucharest in 1913. The demands of

---

192 ibid. p. 249.

193 Source: http://en.wikipedia.org/wiki/Pavel_Shatev, http://mk.wikipedia.org/wiki/ Павел_Шатев, http://bg.wikipedia.org/wiki/ Павел_Шатев, download 17.01.2015)

194 S. Šatev , Makedonskoto nacionalnoosloboditelno dviženje in "Makedonsko delo" No. 11/1926 in D Kartov, os. cit. pp. 251-252.

the VMRO were in accordance with the will of the Macedonian people but certainly not with the policies of the occupying powers. Only in Bulgaria did a section of the VMRO have permission to exist, the so-called "*vrhovisti*". These Macedonians envisaged a future for their country only as part of Bulgaria and did not shirk from using terror and intimidation on their fellow countrymen living in Pirin Macedonia [Bulgaria] to achieve their ends.

Reverting to Greece, the CPG permitted the existence of the VMRO in Aegean Macedonia[195] and soon after, in June 1932, a "*Minority Conference*" was held in Salonika [Mac. Solun] which a CPG delegate, Sklavenas and eleven other representatives of the national minorities attended. The inaugural conference of the VMRO for Aegean Macedonia took place in March 1934 in Voden[196] [Gr. Edhessa] during which it was decided to form local parties. The appearance of the VMRO in Aegean Macedonia was greeted by enthusiasm among Macedonians and thus, according to Andreja Čipov (political leader of the VMRO), 17 local parties with 893 members[197] were founded. The VMRO also achieved success in publishing on the territory of Aegean Macedonia, in Lerin [Gr. Florina] a Macedonian-language newspaper "*The Peasant's Flag*". However, the official CPG paper, *Rizospastis*, printed news in Macedonian but using the Greek alphabet. The local newspaper Nestorion from the town of Nestram published Macedonian folk literature.[198] Another success was the

[195] S Kiselinovski, Egejskiot del na Makedonija 1913–89, Skopje 1969, p. 92 and H Ajdonovski, Vistinata za Egejska Makedonija, Skopje 1971, pp. 60–81.

[196] T Popovski, Makedonskoto nacionalno malcinstvo vo Bugarija, Grcija i Albanija, Skopje 1981, p. 79.

[197] Letter by A Čipov to Dimitar Vlahov, Arhiv na Makedonija, Fond Dimitar Vlahov, k. br. 21(18) in Kiselinovski, os. cit. p. 93.

[198] T Popovski, os. cit. pp. 79–80.

participation of Andreja Čipov in parliamentary elections in 1935. As secretary of the VMRO he wrote under the heading "*Occupation*" in the electoral register, "*Macedonian*".[199]

This recognition of the Macedonian people and the permission to allow the VMRO showed that the CPG had changed its policy. Ideology had given way to reality, thus paving the way for the recognition of other national minorities living in Greece. This policy of equality, adopted by the CPG in 1931 automatically suspended the activities of the VMRO in Aegean Macedonia[200] because now that the CPG recognised and upheld the national rights of the Macedonians,[201] the majority no longer saw any necessity to join the VMRO, particularly as the slogan "*A United and Independent Macedonia*" seemed less important in view of the CPG's guarantee and confirmation of equal rights for all national minorities in Greece. All this constituted a "*natural obstacle*" to the development of the VMRO's activities.

To confirm this new policy, the CPG published a series of articles in "*Rizospastis*". Here is part of the *Resolution* of the VI Plenary Meeting of the Central Committee of the CPG, "*The Situation in Greece and the tasks of the Party*".

> "...to realise the aims of the revolution, namely, land to the peasants, liberating the land from the control of foreign capital, freedom for oppressed nations — the broad masses must be mobilised and united with the proletariat as a first step to a Soviet-style revolution of workers and peasants which will solve all the tasks of a bourgeois-democratic nature and thus be transformed into a true socialist revolution constituting a great victory. In

[199] Letter by A Čipov, ibid.

[200] S Kiselinovski, os. cit. p. 94.

[201] T Popovski, os. cit. p. 80.

order to secure this victory, the Party demands: liberation of the land from the control of foreign capital and dependence on imperialist forces, the repudiation of foreign debts, self-determination for oppressed Macedonians and Thracians, full equality for the Jews.

iii

The most neglected part of the CPG's activities is the issue of the nationalities. Despite objectively favourable conditions for our work among Macedonians and Thracians, the Party has not managed to strengthen its activities in areas inhabited by national minorities or offer help which will serve to promote the aims of the Party with regard to national minorities, both among oppressed nations and the toiling masses.

iv

Serious tasks for the Party

The working classes of the national minorities are the indispensable allies of the working class of Greece in the revolution which is now imminent. It is essential that the Party changes the current reluctance towards working with the national minorities. It is incumbent on us to define the particular means necessary to create and sustain mass communist organisations in the provinces, establish contacts with existing organisations such as the VMRO and the Thracian Revolutionary Organisation. The Party is obliged to carry on an incessant struggle against policies of national oppression, promote the rights of nations to self-determination and separate development and extol the success of the USSR in solving the problem of the
national minorities...

These documents chronicle the complete change of the CPG from denying the problem of national minorities to totally acknowledging it — the demand for equal treatment of national minorities living in Greece, acknowledgement of the Party's neglect towards these minorities, the call for contacts with the *VMRO* and the *Thracian Revolutionary Organisation* - all this showed a fresh understanding of the situation of the national minorities living in Greece. A confirmation of these changes and a recognition of their importance as a basis for Party activities was made at the V Congress of the Party in March 1934. The *Resolution* of the congress is as follows:

1 Revolutionary success and the struggle against fascism and war.

2 Resolution of the Fifth Congress after the Central Committee speech

3 National minorities

> The support and help of the national liberation movements of the national minorities and their organisational strength in the daily struggle against oppression and economic exploitation at the hands of the Greek bourgeoisie as well as the recognition of their rights to self-determination and separate development will enable the CPG to gain their confidence and win proletarian allies for the imminent revolution in our country. The CPG must bring abut the final destruction of Greek nationalism [connected with the "Great Idea"] and eradicate any traces of it in our ranks and promote internationalist awareness amongst workers and peasants"[202]

This *Resolution* also confirms the change in policy towards the national minorities, their rights to self-determination and separation from the Greek state. Through propagating these ideas, the CPG believed it would "*gain their confidence*". But the CPG would change its line again. It would not go back to denying the existence of a Macedonian minority in Greece but it would change the slogan "*United and Independent Macedonia*" into "*Full and equal rights for all minorities*". The change was announced at the VI Congress of the CPG in December 1935. The text concerning Macedonia is as follows:

---

[202] R Kirjazovski, os. cit. pp. 129–130.

"XI. THE MACEDONIAN PROBLEM.

The Political Decision

d and Independent Macedonia" into "Full and equal rights for all minorities". This change in our position towards the national minorities in our country does not indicate a negation of the Marxist-Leninist principles of self-determination for minorities. The change of slogan has taken into account the shifts in the ethnic composition of parts of Greek Macedonia and the new conditions under which the revolutionary movements in our country and in the Balkans are developing which oblige us to combat war and fascism. Marxism-Leninism obliges the Party to adapt its policies and slogans to prevailing conditions. In parts of Macedonia ruled by Greece, many displaced persons from Greece have been re-settled. The population in the Greek parts of Macedonia is now mainly Greek. Leninist-Stalinist principles of self-determination demand that under present conditions we change the old slogan.

The ruling classes, who have a history of selling Greece to foreign imperialists, have sold parts of Greece to the French, the British and the Germans. They have sold and continue to sell the sovereignty of the Greek people. The crowning achievement of their tyrannical policies has been the crushing of the rights by terrorism of the national minorities living in Greece, above all the Macedonians. The CPG's whole-hearted defence of the rights of Macedonians has been branded by the capitalists as *"national betrayal"*. However, the struggle to unmask the class enemy is an extremely urgent matter, especially today when the situation of our country and the development of the Party makes Greece a vital link in the revolutionary movement in the Balkans. We must convince the Greek working class that the Greek bourgeoisie wishes to destroy both Greek freedom movements and the Macedonians in order to perpetuate their hegemony and provoke war in the Balkans. Only fraternal co-operation between the Greek and Macedonian peoples against this common exploitation will bring mutual benefit. The change of slogan certainly does not entail a diminution of our work in Macedonia with national minorities. On the contrary; we shall strengthen our efforts to secure full rights for minorities. The Party will continue to proclaim that the Macedonian problem will be solved after the victory in the Balkans of Soviet power which will tear up the deceitful treaties concerning the exchanges of

> populations and take decisive measures to punish the Imperialists for the crimes they committed in Macedonia. Only then will Macedonia enjoy a full national renaissance."[203]

The *Resolution* of the VI Congress of the CPG confirmed the rights of the Macedonians. The difference lay in the definition of their rights — equality, not national independence. The CPG emphasised however that the change of slogan did not represent "*a subterfuge nor a denial of the Marxist-Leninist principles of self-determination*". Furthermore, they recalled the requirements of political realism, namely that the "*population in the Greek part of Macedonia is now mainly Greek*" which meant that these new conditions "*demanded a change to the old slogan*". They recalled that the Greek bourgeoisie wanted to "*destroy Greek freedom movements and the Macedonians*" but that the only chance of survival was to "*embrace fraternal co-operation between the Greek and Macedonian people*" which would bring "*mutual benefit*". Furthermore they argued that a definitive solution to the Macedonian problem would be reached "*after the victory of Soviet power in the Balkans*" after which "*the Macedonians would enjoy a national renaissance*".

The CPG tried to convince the Comintern of its reasons for changing the slogan. Representatives of the CPG went to Moscow[204] and, armed with the latest statistics concerning the population of Aegean Macedonia, tried to persuade the Polish communist Oskar Walicki, head of the international section for Balkan affairs, to accept the resolutions of the Congress. A high-level meeting was convened, attended by Dmitriy Manuilskiy, Palmiro

---

[203] ibid. pp. 159–160.

[204] S Kiselinovski, os. cit. p. 95.

Togliatti[205], Klement Gottwald[206], Georgi Dimitrov, Wilhelm Pieck[207] and others during which Walicki argued against accepting the resolutions.[208] The Greek delegation was represented by Vasilis Nefeloudhis, Yanis Mihailidhis, Elektra Sidheridhis and Vasilis Bartzotas.[209] The meeting finally decided that the change of slogan was justified. The "*Minority*" faction of the CPG had triumphed over the "*Majority*".

The change of slogan had been justified by the change in the ethnic composition of Aegean Macedonia. But as was shown in the first chapter, the actual situation was different. The question therefore arises, what were the real motives for the CPG's change of policy towards Macedonia? The answer to this question will be attempted in the fifth chapter.

---

205 http://pl.wikipedia.org/wiki/Palmiro_Togliatti, http://en.wikipedia.org/wiki/Palmiro_Togliatti

206 http://pl.wikipedia.org/wiki/Klement_Gottwald, http://en.wikipedia.org/wiki/Klement_Gottwald

207 http://pl.wikipedia.org/wiki/Wilhelm_Pieck, http://en.wikipedia.org/wiki/Wilhelm_Pieck

208 ibid.

209 ibid.

CHAPTER

5

THE REAL REASONS FOR THE GREEK COMMUNIST PARTY'S CHANGE OF POLICY TOWARDS THE SLOGAN OF A "UNITED AND INDEPENDENT MACEDONIA"

The reasons for the change in the CPG's position towards the concept of a "*United and Independent Macedonia*" were twofold; internal and external, each of which influenced the other and resulted in the CPG's rejection of the policy supporting a united and independent Macedonia and an acceptance of equal rights for all minorities within a Greek state.[210] We shall consider the external factors first. They were of particular importance and very powerfully influenced the CPG's change of policy. Immediately after the establishment of a "*new European Versailles*", a whole series of national and territorial problems were created because the new states frequently did not fit into the boundaries of the old states they superseded. In addition, a wave of revolutionary movements occurred between 1917 and 1923 which alarmed the European bourgeoisie and prompted them to abandon liberalism and move increasingly towards totalitarianism. The bourgeoisie demanded a system of government

---

[210] S Kiselinovski, Egejskiot del na Makedonija (1913–89), Skopje 1990, p. 98.

which would provide the stability necessary for their economic interests and so gradually dictatorial governments began to come to power in Europe; Italy,[211] Spain,[212] Portugal,[213] Hungary,[214] Austria,[215] Estonia,[216] Poland.[217] The trend culminated in the fascist dictatorship of Adolf Hitler in Germany[218] and as a result, the border agreements signed at Versailles began to unravel; in Denmark, Belgium, France, Czechoslovakia and Poland. Germany began to support German national movements in Poland (Silesia and Danzig/Gdańsk) in Czechoslovakia (Sudetenland) and Romania (Transylvania) In effect, fascism began to spread in these countries as well as to Austria, incorporated into the Reich in March 1938.[219] The whole post–Versailles settlement was put into question. The revisionist policies of Germany with their strongly anti-Communist sentiments began to influence the policies of the Comintern, particularly as fascism began to spread more and more widely to other countries. The Comintern's global strategy thus began to undergo fundamental change.

---

211 J A Gierowski, Historia Włoch, Wrocław 1985, pp. 573–592. See also S Sierpowski, Faszyzm we Włoszech, Wrocław 1973.

212 G I J Moch, Rewolucja w Hiszpanii, Księgarnia M Fruchtmana, Warszawa 1935, 5 pp. 328–330, p .660–669. Vilar, Historia Hiszpanii, PWN, Warszawa 1991, pp. 92–96.

213 A H de Oliveira Marques, Historii Portugalii, vol. 2, Warszawa, pp. 336–352.

214 See W Felczak, Historia Węgier, Wrocław Wrocław 1983, pp. 328–330.

215 H Wereszycki, Historia Austrii, Wrocław 1986, pp. 293–296.

216 See J W Borejsza, Rzym a wspólnota faszystowska, Warszawa 1981.

217 A Ajnenkiel, Od rządów ludowych do przewrotu majowego, Warszawa 1977 and Polska po przewrocie majowym, Warszawa 1980.

218 See W Czapliński, A Gajos, W Korta, Historia Niemiec, Wrocław 1990. Also F Ryszka, Państwo stanu wyjątkowego, Wrocław 1990, pp. 660–669.

219 W Wereszycki, op. cit. pp. 297–298.

The fascist policies of territorial expansion and ideological subversion had to be met by equally effective communist counter-measures in which the USSR had a vital interest in the face of threats to its national and ideological integrity. The Comintern thus began to lend more and more support to the National Front. The most lucid statement of this policy was given by Georgi Dimitrov in a speech entitled "*Fascism and the Working Class*" given at the VII Congress of the Comintern in Moscow in 1935.

" The denial of victory to fascism depends above all on the combat abilities of the working class whose strength is incorporated into a fighting army waging war on capitalism and fascism. If the proletariat achieves unity in its fighting ranks, it will weaken the influence of fascism on the peasantry, the urban lower middle classes, youth and the intelligentsia, neutralise some of them and win over the rest to its cause.

Secondly, the existence of a powerful revolutionary party is essential to lead the struggle of the toiling masses against fascism. If the Party exhorts workers to sound the retreat in the face of fascism and allows the fascist bourgeoisie to strengthen its position, this Party will assuredly lead the workers to defeat.

Thirdly, it is necessary to formulate a correct policy of the working class towards the peasantry and urban lower middle classes. The masses should be treated as they are, not as we would like them to be. Only in their struggle will they be able to conquer their doubts, only in painful confrontation with their own understandable hesitations and with the political backing of the proletariat will they be able to move onto a higher plane of revolutionary consciousness and activity. Fourthly, the vigilance and correct timing of proletarian activities is of utmost importance. We must deny fascism the advantage of surprise, never allow it to gain the initiative and ensure that we deliver the decisive blows and never allow it to regain its strength, resist it at every step wherever it rears its head, prevent it from taking up new positions just as the French proletariat are currently doing.

These are the most important ways of preventing the spread of fascism and its access to power".[220]

As is evident from the text, the opposition to fascism came from the grass roots of society, the workers and peasants. The Party demanded a "*fighting army*" as well as "*denying fascism the advantage of surprise*". Furthermore, Dimitrov emphasised that the masses should be treated "*as they are and not as we would like them to be*".

Returning to the former policy of the Comintern and its resolutions of the 1924 Congress, it was stated that the presence of minorities in countries whose territorial integrity was under threat would weaken them. This would be detrimental to the Party's fight against fascism. The Communist parties of the Balkans have to oppose fascism in one way only, namely by pursuing a judicious policy towards the question of the national minorities in those countries and thus protect them from revisionist tendencies.

The previous slogan of a "United and Independent Macedonia" was in contradiction to the new global policy of the Comintern. Not disintegration but unity was the means to combat fascism. National questions had to be settled within the framework of already existing Balkan states. This policy was

[220] Faszyzmy europejskie w oczach współczesnych i historyków, Warszawa 1979, pp. 161–162.

convenient for the CPG because it did not provoke opposition from its rank and file as did the previous slogan.

As far as internal factors were concerned, these were few. The first was the total lack of interest and even reluctance on the part of the Greeks to accept the slogan "*United and Independent Macedonia*". This applied both to the inhabitants of so-called "*Old Greece*" [Sterea Elladha] and to immigrants from Asia Minor [Modern Turkey and the Caucasus]. Neither the one nor the other were in the least interested in an independent Macedonian state separate from Greece. Because of this, the CPG had no support in Greece; it was deemed a party of "*national traitors*". To change this state of affairs, the slogan "*United and Independent Macedonia*" had to be changed to "*Full and Equal Rights for Minorities*" in order to win back support of the Greek workers and peasants. As it was, the lives of such people were hard enough and communist slogans promising equality and social justice always fell on fertile soil.

The second internal factor was the continuous struggle between the "*Minority*" and the "*Majority*" factions in the CPG. Despite the formal dominance of the "*Majority*" over the "*Minority*", in the end, the "*Minority*" prevailed because they reflected more accurately the aspirations of the Greek people — the dream of a strong, re-born Greek state whose "*lost*" lands in Turkey would be compensated for by "*regained*" lands in Macedonia and Thrace. Hence the "*Majority's*" desire to implement the resolutions of the V Congress of the Comintern in 1924 was not popular among the leading figures of the CPG but in the end their attempts to force the "*Minority*" to abandon the aim of creating an independent Macedonian state were crowned with success at the VI Congress of the CPG in December 1935.

The third factor was that a large part of the "*Majority*" regarded Macedonia as a tactical rather than central issue. This meant that the Comintern's resolutions for Macedonia were accepted but only under protest and against the will of the CPG. In addition, the run-up to Greek parliamentary elections caused the issue to be down-played. Votes were gained from Macedonians who were sympathetic to the CPG but later the issue was side-lined so as not to arouse misgivings amongst Greeks in general.

The fourth factor was the awareness in every Greek of the "*Great Idea*". When the Greek state was founded in 1830, the Greek bourgeoisie began to promote the idea of expanding Greek territory. To this end, they began to propagate the idea amongst the Greeks that the territories of Asia Minor, Thrace, Macedonian and Southern Albania had always been Greek, both historically and ethnically. There was of course not a grain of truth in these assertions but this did not prevent them from implanting the idea that "*Greater Greece*" consisted of all lands between the Adriatic, the Black Sea and the Mediterranean.

Members of the CPG breathed the atmosphere of "*Greater Greece*". Whether they wanted to or not, creating a party with a different ideological content would still not be able to exclude from its agenda what the Greeks were taught in school, what they heard in the streets, what they all subconsciously believed in — a "*Greater Greece*". The idea therefore of an independent Macedonia, even amongst the rank and file of the Party and the people, would be very hard to accept for it would be tantamount to national betrayal.

All these factors combined to create the impetus to change the slogan "*United and Independent Macedonia*" to "*Full and Equal Rights for Minorities*". In addition, there emerged a belief that by changing the slogan, the CPG would succeed in winning over the Greeks as a whole to the fight agains fascism.[221] Rejecting a "*United and Independent Macedonia*" was seen as the most effective means to achieve this end.

[221] On all these matters see the memoirs of Macedonian partisan leaders in Aegean Macedonia in V Ajanovski-Oče, Egejski buri, Skopje 1975. http://en.wikipedia.org/wiki/Vangel_Ajanovski-Oče.

APPENDIX I

GREEK ACTS AGAINST THE MACEDONIANS (1912 - 1994)

By Peter Medichkov

The following chronicles the methods employed by Greece in its effort to eradicate the centuries old Macedonian ethnic presence in Aegean Macedonia (Greek-Macedonia) in the name of Greek territorial expansion. Specific laws and decrees are presented against the backdrop of relevant historical events affecting Macedonians in Aegean Macedonia.

The chronology begins in 1912 when Greece, for the first time ever, came into possession of Macedonian territory and this by force of arms, almost a decade after the 1903 Ilinden (St. Ilija Day) Uprising lead by the IMRO (Internal Macedonian Revolutionary Organization) in a failed effort to free Macedonia from the Ottoman yoke.

The ominous prophecy of Harilaos Trikoupis, Greek Prime Minister from 1882 to 1895, foretold what the neighboring Greek state had in mind for Macedonia and its people:

"When the great war comes, Macedonia will become Greek or Bulgarian, according to who wins. If it is taken by the Bulgarians, they will take the population Slavs. If we take it, we will make all of them Greeks".

1912 BALKAN WARS

Irredentist Greece, Serbia, Bulgaria and Montenegro drive a crumbling Ottoman Empire out of the Balkans and pursue territorial expansion into Macedonia. Greek army enters Aegean Macedonia ostensibly to "liberate" Macedonia from the Ottoman.

1913

Greek, Serbian, Bulgarian alliance breaks down over competing claims for Macedonia. Bulgaria miscalculates and attacks Serbia and Greek armies. Ottoman forces rejoin war against Bulgaria. Bulgaria defeated, loses territorial gains in Macedonia.

From "liberation to tyranny", Greek army commences savage and bloody "ethnic cleansing" of the towns of Kukush, Doiran, Demir-Hisar and Serres in the Aegean Macedonia.

160 Macedonian villages burned, and atrocities committed. Mass exodus of refugees.

Treaty of Bucharest (Aug. 10, 1913), ends War and partitions Macedonia.

Greece refers to conquered Macedonian lands as the "new territories" under "military administration". Not yet officially incorporated into the Kingdom of Greece.

Military occupation augmented by influx of administrators, educators; police brought from Greece.

Professor R.A. Reiss reports to the Greek government: "Those whom you would call Bulgarian speakers I would simply call Macedonians... Macedonian is not the language they speak in Sofia...I repeat the mass of inhabitants there (Macedonia) remain simply Macedonians."

1917

LAW 1051 Greece inaugurates new administrative jurisdictions for governing newly acquired lands in Aegean Macedonia.

1919 TREATY OF VERSAILLES (PARIS)

England and France ratify the principles of the Bucharest Treaty and endorse the partitioning of Macedonia.

Greece pursues forced expulsion and denationalization of Macedonians and begins colonization by transplanting "Greeks" into Aegean Macedonia.

Article 51 of Treaty of Versailles espouses equality of civil rights, education, language, and religion for all national minorities which Greece violates and ignores.

Neuilly Convention and forced exchange of populations. About 70,000 Macedonians expelled from Aegean Macedonia to Bulgaria and 25,000

THE COMMUNIST PARTY OF GREECE AND THE MACEDONIAN NATIONAL PROBLEM 1918–1940

Greeks transplanted from Bulgaria to Aegean Macedonia.

Greek Commission on Toponyms issues instructions for choosing Hellenized names for Macedonian places in the Aegean Macedonia.

1920

Greek Ministry Of Internal Affairs publishes booklet: Advice on the Change of the Names of Municipalities and Villages in Aegean Macedonia.

1925

76 names of Macedonian villages and towns in the Aegean Macedonia Hellenized since 1918 by Greek authorities.

LEAGUE OF NATIONS pressures Greece to extend rights to Macedonian minority.

ABECEDAR Primer printed in Athens for use by Macedonian school children in Aegean Macedonia. Written in Latin alphabet and reflect the Macedonian spoken in Lerin district in western Aegean Macedonia.

Serbs and Bulgarians protest to League of Nations. Primer undermines their claim that Macedonians are Serbs and Bulgarians respectively.

Greece counters with last minute cable to League: "the population... knows neither the Serbian nor the Bulgarian language and speaks nothing but a Slav-Macedonian idiom."

Greece "retreats" so as to preserve Balkan alliances. Primer is destroyed after League of Nations delegates leave Solun/Salonica. Thereafter, Greece denies existence of Macedonians. Refers to Macedonians as "Slavophone Greeks", "Old Bulgarians" and many other appellations but not as Macedonians.

1926

Legislative Orders in Government Gazette #331 orders Macedonian names of towns, villages, mountains changed to Greek names.

1927

Cyrillic inscriptions destroyed or overwritten from churches, tombstones and icons. Church services in the Macedonian language are outlawed.

Macedonians Ordered To Abandon Personal Names And Under Duress Adopt Greek Names Assigned To Them By The Greek State.

1928

1, 497 Macedonian place-names in the Aegean Macedonia Hellenized since 1926.

English Journalist V. Hild reveals, "The Greeks do not only persecute living Slavs (Macedonians)..., but they even persecute dead ones. They do not leave them in peace even in the graves. They erase the Slavonic inscriptions on the headstones, remove the bones and burn them."

1929

Greek government enacts law where any demands for national rights By Macedonians are regarded as high treason.

LAW 4096 directive on renaming Macedonian place-names.

1936

Reign of terror by fascist dictator General Metaxas, 1936-40. Macedonians suffer state terrorism and pogroms.

Thousands of Macedonians jailed, sent to internal exile (EXORIA) on arid, inhospitable Greek islands, where many perish. Their crime? Being ethnic Macedonian by birth.
LAW 6429 reinforces Law 4096 on Hellenization of toponyms.
DECREE 87 accelerates denationalization of Macedonians.
Greek ministry of Education sends "Specially trained" instructors to accelerate conversion to Greek language.

1938

LAW 23666 bans the use of the Macedonian language and strives to erase every trace of the Macedonian identity.
Macedonians fined, beaten, jailed for speaking Macedonian. Adults and school children further humiliated by being forced to drink castor oil when caught speaking Macedonian.
LAW 1418 reinforces previous laws on renamings.

1940

39 more place-names Hellenized since 1929.

1945

LAW 697 more regulations on renaming toponyms in the Aegean Macedonia.

THE COMMUNIST PARTY OF GREECE AND THE MACEDONIAN NATIONAL PROBLEM 1918–1940

1947

LAW L-2 citizens suspected of opposing Greek government in civil War stripped of their citizenship, including relatives, arbitrarily and without due process.

1948

LAW M properties confiscated from citizens who fought against

government and those accused of assisting.
28,000 Child Refugees, mostly Macedonians, from areas of heavy fighting evacuated to Yugoslavia, Czechoslovakia, Poland, Hungary, Bulgaria and Romania. Greece denies their right of return to this day.
RESOLUTION 193C(III) United Nations Resolution calls for repatriation to Greece of Child Refugees.

U.N. UNIVERSAL DECLARATION OF HUMAN RIGHTS ARTICLE 19: Everyone has the right to freedom of opinion and expression; this right includes freedom to hold opinions without interference and to seek, receive an impart information and ideas through any media and regardless of frontiers.
DECREE 504 continues property confiscations of exiles and colonization of Aegean Macedonia with people from Turkey, Egypt and other parts of Greece. Parcels of land given to colonists along with financial incentives.

1959
LAW 3958 allows confiscation of property of those who left Greece and did not return within five years.
Several villages in the Aegean Macedonia forced to swear “Language oaths” to speak only Greek and renounce their mother tongue (Macedonian).

1962
DECREE 4234 reinforces past laws regarding confiscated properties of political exiles and denies them right to return.

1968
EUROPEAN COMMISSION ON HUMAN RIGHTS accuses Greece of human rights abuses.

1969

COUNCIL OF EUROPE declares Greece "undemocratic, illiberal, authoritarian, and oppressive". Greece forced to resign from Council of Europe under threat of expulsion.

Military Junta continues the policy of colonizing the confiscated lands in Aegean Macedonia. Land handled over to persons with a "proven patriotism" for Greece.

EUROPEAN CONVENTION FOR THE PROTECTION OF HUMAN RIGHTS AND FREEDOMS signed by Greece states: ARTICLE 10(1) Everyone has the right to freedom of expression. This right shall include freedom to hold opinions and to receive and impart information and ideas without interference by public authority and regardless of frontiers.

1976

DECREE 233 suspends about 150 past decrees, government decisions and laws since 1913. Regulations for the confiscation of properties belonging to Macedonian political exiles not affected.

1979

135 places renamed in the Aegean Macedonia since 1940. The Greek vigil regarding names is an indicator of the Macedonian ethnic identity in the Aegean Macedonia.

1982

Greek internal security police urges intensive campaign to wipe out remaining Macedonian language and consciousness in the Aegean Macedonia.

LAW 106841 political exiles who fled during the Civil War and were stripped of their citizenship are allowed to return providing they are "Greek by ethnic origin". The same rights are denied to Macedonian political exiles born in the Aegean Macedonia.

U.N. UNIVERSAL DECLARATION OF HUMAN RIGHTS ARTICLE 17,

No one can be deprived of his own property against his will.

1985

DECREE 1540, Political exiles who fled during Civil War allowed to reclaim confiscated lands provided they are "Greeks by ethnic origin". Same rights denied to Macedonian exiles born in the Aegean Macedonia.

THE COMMUNIST PARTY OF GREECE AND THE MACEDONIAN NATIONAL PROBLEM 1918–1940

U.N. UNIVERSAL DECLARATION OF HUMAN RIGHTS ARTICLE 13.

Everyone has the right to leave any country, including his own, as well as to return to his own country.

1986

International writers' organization, PEN, condemns Greece's denial of the existence of Macedonians and their language.

Greece escalates climate of fear in Aegean Macedonia.

Greece officially calls the Republic of Macedonia as the Republic of "Skopje", after the name of its capital city; and Macedonians are called "Skopjans".

The term "Skopjans" used to label Greek citizens who declare themselves as ethnic Macedonians. "Skopjans" laced with hatred, and racism. It connotes a traitor to Hellenism.

1990

CSCE COPENHAGEN CONFERENCE ON THE HUMAN DIMENSION, to which Greece is a signatory, states in ARTICLE 32: "Persons belonging to national minorities have the right freely to express, preserve, and develop their ethnic, cultural, linguistic, or religious identity and to maintain and develop their culture in all its aspects, free of any attempts as assimilation against their will". ARTICLE 33: "Participating states will protest the ethnic, cultural, linguistic and religious identity of national minorities...and create conditions for the

promotion of that identity".
GREEK HIGH COURT DECISION 19, refuses registration of "CENTER FOR MACEDONIAN CULTURE" in Florina. Appeal is turned down by High Appeals Court, in Salonika. Further appeal dismissed by Supreme Administrative Council of Greece in Athens.

1991

CSCE MEETING ON NATIONAL MINORITIES IN GENEVA, in which Greece participated states: "Issues concerning national minorities... are matters of legitimate international concern and consequently do not constitute exclusively an internal affair of the respective State... Participating States reaffirm, and will not hinder the exercise of, the right of persons belonging to national minorities to establish and maintain their own educational, cultural and religious institutions, organizations and associations". Belligerent anti-Macedonian propaganda incites Greek population into a state of chauvinistic hysteria.

Translation from Greek: "Hang the Skopje Gypsies"

1992

Greece and Serbia conspire to overthrow and partition the Republic of Macedonia.

1993

Macedonian human rights activists Hristos Sidhiropoulos and Tasos Boulis were prosecuted under Greek Panel Code: Article 36, Para 191; disseminating false information; Para 192; inciting citizens to disturb the peace. Their crime? Declaring themselves as Macedonians in interview for Greek magazine ENA.

Macedonian human rights activist and priest Nikodimos Tsarknias derobed and expelled by Greek Orthodox Church because of his human rights activities. Tsarknias refused a Greek bribe which would have elevated him to bishop in 1989. Threatened with death.

1994

Extremists in Australia's Greek Community burn two Macedonian churches, after Australian recognition of Macedonia.

Greece continues to deny the existence of Macedonians in Aegean Macedonia despite overwhelming evidence to the contrary.

Greece continues repressive and unrelenting policies against Macedonians in Aegean Macedonia despite objections by international human rights organizations.

BIBLIOGRAPHY

Note: In this bibliography, the author has provided English translations of Polish and Macedonian titles for English speakers.

I. PUBLISHED DOCUMENTS

Borejsza, JW (ed.) 1979, Faszyzmy europejskie 1922–1945 w oczach współczesnych i historyków (European fascisms 1922–1945 in the eyes of modern men and historians),Warsaw.

Kirjazovski, R 1982, KPG i makedonskoto nacionalno prašanje 1918–1974 (The CPG and the Macedonian national question 1918–1974), Skopje.

II. MEMOIRS, RECOLLECTIONS.

Ajanovski-Oče, V 1975, Egejski buri (Aegean storms), Skopje.

III. BOOKS AND ARTICLES.

Aarbake, V 2003, 'Ethnic rivalry and the Quest for Macedonia (1870–1913)', East European Monographs, Boulder, (distr. by Columbia University Press), New York.

Aegean part of Macedonia after the Balkan Wars, Council for Research into South–Eastern Europe of the Macedonian Academy of Sciences and Arts, <http://www.historyofmacedonia.org/MacedonianMinorities/AegeanMacedonia.htm>.

Ajnenkiel, A 1977, Od rządów ludowych do przewrotu majowego (From the people's rule till the May coup), Warszawa.

——1980, Polska po przewrocie majowym (Poland after the May coup), Warszawa.

Aleksoski, V 1993, Vistinata za Makedonija niz francuskata istoriografija (The truth about Macedonia in the French historiography), Skopje.

Amnesty International 1993, Greece: Torture and ill-treatment, London, January.

Anastasoff, Ch 1938, The tragic peninsula. A history of the Macedonia Movement for Independence since 1878, St. Louise.

Anastasovski, N 2008, The contest for Macedonian identity 1870-1912, Pollitecon Publications, Sydney.

Andonov-Poljanski, H 1978, Goce Delčev i negovoto vreme (Goce Delčev and his times), Kultura, Skopje.

——1990, Makedonskoto prašanje (The Macedonian question), Skopje.

Andonovski, H 1971, Vistinata za Egejska Makedonija (The truth about Aegean Macedonia), Skopje.

——1968, Makedoncite pod Grcija vo borbata protiv fašizmot 1940–44 (The Macedonians under Greece in the struggle against fascism 1940–44), Skopje,

——1993, Greek evidence on the authenticity of the Macedonians, Macedonian Review, 1/1993, Skopje. <http://www.historyofmacedonia.org/MacedonianGreekConflict/GreekEvidence.html>

'Armistice of Mudanya', Wikipedia, <http://en.wikipedia.org/wiki/Armistice_of_Mudanya>

'Atatürk Kemal', Wikipedia, <http://en.wikipedia.org/wiki/Kemal_Ataturk> , http://www.turkishembassy.org.au/ataturk/ataturk.htm

Baer, MD 2010, The Dönme: Jewish Converts, Muslim Revolutionaries, and Secular Turks, Stanford University Press, Stanford.

Batowski, H 1988, Między dwiema wojnami 1919–1939 (Between two wars 1919–1939), Kraków.

——1938, Państwa Bałkańskie 1800–1923 (The Balkan states 1800–1923), Kraków.

——1982, Rozpad Austro–Węgier 1914–1918 (Break-up of Austo–Hungary 1914–1918), Kraków.

'Battle of Dumlupinar', Wikipedia, <http://en.wikipedia.org/wiki/Battle_of_Dumlupinar>

'Battle of Sakarya', Wikipedia, < http://en.wikipedia.org/wiki/Battle_of_Sakarya>

Bazylow, L 1985, Historia Rosji (2005 wyd. IV, poprawione i uzupełnione) (History of Russia),(4th edn corrected and updated by Wieczorkiewicz and published in 2005), Ossolineum,Wrocław.

'Benaroya Avraam', Wikipedia, http://en.wikipedia.org/wiki/Avraam_Benaroya

Bitovski, K 2001, Grčkata "Makedonska borba 1904–1908", (The Greek "Macedonian struggle 1904-1908"), Skopje.

Bogos, V & Bogov, V (n. d.), Macedonian revelation: historical documents rock and shatter modern political ideology, V & D Bogov Publishers, 127 Coode Street, Bayswater, Western Australia 6053.

Bonarek J, Czekalski T, Sprawski S, Turlej S, Historia Grecji, 2005,Kraków.

Borejsza, JW 1981, Rzym a wspólnota faszystowska (Rome and the fascist community), Warszawa.

Bozcaada, <http://tr.wikipedia.org/wiki/Bozcaada>

Brailsford, HN 1906, Macedonia: its races and their future, Methuen & Co., London. [The author of this book does not distinguish the Macedonians from the Bulgarians. The book was written in 1906 when most of the Western authors did the same mistake caused by a fact that the Macedonians did not have their own church and participated in services performed by the Bulgarian, Serbian or Greek prists. In most cases it decided how the Macedonians were recognized and treated. Also the similarity between the Bulgarian and the Macedonia language which for the Western authors sounded the same where another factor combined with the Bulgarian propaganda which "proved" the thesis that the "Bulgarians" live in Macedonia], <http://knigite.abv.bg/en/hb/index.html>

Brown, K 2003, Macedonia's Child–Grandfathers: the transnational politics of memory, excile, and return, 1948–1998, The Henry M. Jackson School of International Studies, University of Washington, no. 38.

Brzeziński, A M 2002, Grecja (Greece), Wyd. Trio, Warszawa.

Budziszewska, W 1983, Słownik bałkanizmów w dialektach Macedonii Egejskiej (Dictionary of balakanisms in the dialects of Aegean Macedonia), Wydawnictwa Uniwersytetu Warszawskiego, Warszawa.

Carabott, P 2005, 'Aspects of the Hellenization of Greek Macedonia, ca 1912—ca 1959', Kampos: Cambridge papers in Modern Greek, no. 13.

Čašule, I 1990, Let's learn Macedonian (with 3000 word Macedonia-English dictionary). Macquarie University, School of Modern Languages, Sydney.

Chlebowczyk, J 1998, Między dyktatem, realiami a prawem do samostanowienia (Between a dictate, realities and the right to self-determination), PWN, Warszawa.

Clogg, R (ed) 1976, The Movement for Greek Independence, London.

——2006, Historia Grecji nowożytnej (A short history of Modern Greece), Książka i Wiedza, Warszawa.

Cole, GDH 1958, A history of socialist thought, Macmillan, London.

'Communist Party of Greece', Wikipedia, <http://en.wikipedia.org/wiki/KKE>

Connor, W 1984, The national question in Marxist–Leninist theory and strategy, Prinston University Press, New Jersey.

Czamańska I, Szulc W, Pojęcie Macedonii i Macedończyków w ciągu wieków (A concept of Macedonia and Macedonians throughout centuries), 2002, in: Wokół Macedonii: siła kultury – kultura siły (red. B. Zieliński), UAM, Poznań.

Czapliński W, Galos A, & Korta W 1990, Historia Niemiec (History of Germany), Ossolineum, Wrocław.

Czekalski T 2007, Pogrobowcy Wielkiej Idei (Epigones of the Great Idea), Kraków.

Czekanowski, J 1927, Wstęp do historji Słowian (Introduction to the history of Slavs), K.S. Jakubowski, Lwów.

——1948, Polska–Słowiańszczyzna: perspektywy antropologiczne (Poland–Slavic lands: anthropological perspective), Warszawa.

Dakin, D 1966, The Greek struggle in Macedonia 1897-1013, Institute for Balkan Studies,Thessaloniki.

——1972, The unification of Greece 1870-1923, Ernst Benn Limited, London.

Dancig, B 1949, Turcija (Turkey), Voiennoie Izdatel'stvo Ministierstva Vooružiennych Sił Sojuza SSR, Moskva.

Demel, J 1986, Historia Rumunii (History of Romania), Wrocław.

De Oliveira Marques, AH 1987, Historia Portugalii (History of Portugal), vol. 2, Warszawa.

'Dhimotiki', Wikipedia, <http://en.wikipedia.org/wiki/Modern_Greek>

Dimeski, D 1992, Goce Delčev, Skopje.

Dimevski, S 1989, Istorija na makedonskata pravoslavna crkva (The history of the Macedonian Orthodox Church), Skopje.

Documents on the history of the Greek Jews, 1999, Ministry of Foreign Affairs of Greece, University of Athens, Kastaniotis Editions, Athens.

Donev, J 1988, Golemite sili i Makedonija za vreme na Prvata balkanska vojna (The super powers and Macedonia during the First Balkan War), Skopje.

Dural, A. B 2007, His story: Mustafa Kemal and Turkish Revolution, iUniverse, Inc.New York.

Džikov, S 1991, Progoneti (Expelled Macedonians), Skopje.

——1994, Makedonija vo komunističkiot triagolnik (Macedonia in the communist triangle), Nezavisni izdanija, 29, NIP G'urg'a, Skopje.

Elliniki Ekpaidevtiki Enkiklopedia, 1993, Athens.

Enghromi Enkiklopedia Idhroghios, 1982, Ekdhosis Dhomiki, Athens.

Ege Adaları, <http://tr.wikipedia.org/wiki/Ege_Adalar%C4%B1>

'Exchange of population between Greece and Turkey', Wikipedia, <http://en.wikipedia.org/wiki/Exchange_of_populations_between_Greece _and_Turkey>

Felczak, W 1983, Historia Węgier (History of Hungary), Ossolineum,Wrocław.

Friedman, V 2001, Macedonian grammar , <http//www.seelrc.org:8080/grammar/mainframe.jsp?nLanguageID=3 >, SEELRC

From war to Whittlesea: oral histories of Macedonian child refugees, 1999, Macedonian Welfare Workers' Network of Victoria, Pollitecon Publications.

Gaber, V 2008, Recognition and denial. Greece and the Macedonians after Versailles, Sydey.

Gandeto, JSG 2002, Ancient Macedonians: differences between the ancient Macedonians and the ancient Greeks, Writer's Showcase, an imprint of iUniverse Inc.

Gierowski, JA 1985, Historia Włoch (History of Italy), Ossolineum, Wrocław.

Giza, A 1996, Ziemie macedońskie na przełomie XIX i XX wieku (Macedonian lands at the turn of XIX and XX century), Uniwersytet Szczeciński, Szczecin.

—— 1998, Państwa bałkańskie wobec kwestii macedońskiej w latach 1878–1918 (The Balkan states towards the Macedonian question in the years1878–1918) , Uniwersytet Szczeciński, Szczecin.

—— 2001, Stosunki narodowościowe na ziemiach macedońskich na początku XX wieku (National relations on Macedonian lands in the beginning of XX century), Balcanica Posnaniensia XI/XII, UAM, Poznań.

Gleny, M 2000, The Balkans 1804–1999: nationalism, war and the Great Powers, Granta Books. London 2000.

Gökçeada, <http://tr.wikipedia.org/wiki/G%C3%B6k%C3%A7eada,_%C3%87anak kale>

'Great Fire of Smyrna', Wikipedia, <http://en.wikipedia.org/wiki/Great_Fire_of_Smyrna>

'Greco-Turkish War (1919-1922)', Wikipedia, <http://en.wikipedia.org/wiki/Greco-Turkish_War_(1919-1922)>

Greece against its Macedonia minority: the "Rainbow" trial, 1998, Greek Helsinki Monitor & Minority Rights Group–Greece. ETEPE. Athens, <www.greekhelsinki.gr>

'Greek Civil War', Wikipedia, <http://en.wikipedia.org/wiki/Greek_Civil_War>

Greek foreign policy documents , <http://www.macedonian-heritage.gr/Official Documents /index.html>

Greek history <http://commons.wikimedia.org/wiki/File:Greekhistory.GIF>.

'Greek struggle for Macedonia', Wikipedia, <http://en.wikipedia.org/wiki/Greek_Struggle_for_Macedonia>.

'Greek War of Independence', Wikipedia, <http://en.wikipedia.org/wiki/Greek_War_of_Inde-pendence>.

Harbord, J 1920, Conditions in the Near East: Report of the American Military Mission to Armenia. Government Printing Office, Washington.

Holden, D 1972, Greece without columns: the making of the modern Greece, J. B. Lippincott Co., Philadelphia and New York.

Horbal, B 2004, Sprawa łemkowska na konferencji pokojowej w Paryżu w 1919 roku (The Lemko question at the Peace Conference in Paris in 1919), Wrocławskie Studia Wschodnie 8 (2004), WUW.

Human Rights Watch 1994, Denying ethnic identity: The Macedonians of Greece, Human Rights Watch, New York, Washington, Los Angeles, London, <http://www.hrw.org/reports/pdfs/g/greece/greece945.pdf>

Hupnick, DP 2002, The Balkans: from Constantinople to communism, Palgrave. New York.

Ilindensko–Preobraženskoto vystanie ot 1903 godina (Ilinden–Preobražen Uprising of 1903), 1983, Izdatelstvo na Bylgarska Akademija na Naukite, Sofija.

'Imbros and Tenedos', Wikipedia, <http://en.wikipedia.org/wiki/Imbros_and_Tenedos>

Istorija na Makedonskijot narod (The history of the Macedonia nation) 1969, (book 2 and 3), Skopje.

Jewish Holocaust Victims of Thessaloniki (Salonika), <http://www.sephardicstudies.org/thess.html>

'Jews in Greece', Wikipedia, <http://en.wikipedia.org/wiki/Greek_Jews>

Jön Türkler, <http://tr.wikipedia.org/wiki/J%C3%B6n_T%C3%BCrkler>

Kahl, T 2002, The ethnicity of Aromanians after 1990: the identity of a minority that behaves like a majority, Ethnologia Balcanica, Vol. 6.

Karakasidou, A 1997, Fields of wheat, hills of blood: passages to nationhood in Greek Macedonia 1870–1990, University of Chicago Press, Chicago.

'Karamanli(des)', Wikipedia, <http://en.wikipedia.org/wiki/Karamanlides>

Kartov, V, 1987, Makedonskiot narod i pravoto na samoopredeluvanje 1912-1941, Skopje.

'Katharevousa', Wikipedia, <http://en.wikipedia.org/wiki/Katharevousa>

Kirjazovski, R 1989, Makedonskata politička emigracija od Egejskiot del na Makedonija vo istočnoevropskite zemji po Vtorata svetska vojna (The Macedonian political emigration from the Aegean part of Macedonia in East European countries after the Second World War), Skopje.

——1991, Makedonski nacionalni institucii vo Egejskiot del na Makedonija 1941–1961 (Macedonian national institutions in the Aegean part of Macedonia 1991–1961), Skopje.

——1991, Demokratski i antifašistički partii i organizacii vo Egejskiot del na Makedonija 1941–1945 (Democratic and anti–fascist parties and organizations in the Aegean part of Macedonia 1941–1945), Skopje.

——1998, Makedonskoto nacionalno prašanje i Grag'anskata vojna vo Grcija (The Macedonian national cause and the Civil War in Greece), Skopje.

——2000, Afirmacijata na nacionalniot identitet na Makedoncite vo egejskiot del na Makedonija (The affirmation of the national identity of the

Macedonians in the Aegean part of Macedonia), Glasnik, yearbook.44. no.1, Skopje.

——2001, Egejskiot del na Makedonija po Grag'anskata vojna vo Grcija (Aegean Macedonia after the Civil War in Greece), Skopje.

Kiselinovski, S 1985, KPG i makedonskoto nacionalno prašanje 1918–1940 godina (CPG and the Macedonian national question 1918–1940), Skopje.

——1990, Egejskiot del na Makedonija 1913–1989 (Aegean part of Macedonia 1913–1989), Skopje.

——1998, Makedonija niz vekovite (Macedonia through the centuries; I Makedhonia ana tous aiones), Skopje.

——2000, Etničkite promeni vo Makedonija (1913–1995) (Ethnic changes in Macedonia (1913–1995)), Skopje.

——& Stawowy–Kawka, I 2004, Malcinstvata na Balkanot (Minorities in the Balkans), Skopje.

——2007, Istorija na Makedonija (A history of Macedonia),Menora, Skopje.

——2017, Istorija na sovremena Grcija (A history of modern Greece), Menora, Skopje.

Kitchen, M 1992, Historia Europy 1919 – 1939 (Europe between the wars), Wrocław.

Kofos, E 1989, Nationalism & Communism in Macedonia, Caratzas, New York.

Kołodziejczyk, D 2000, Turcja (Turkey), Wydawnictwo Trio, Warszawa.

Koneski, B 1986, Istorija na makedonskiot jazik (The history of the Macedonian language), Skopje.

Kosmala, G 1993, Zmiany granic politycznych w Europie środkowej w okresie ostatnich stu lat (The change of political borders in Central Europe in the period of the last 100 years), Wrocław.

Kostopoulos, T 2000, I apaghorevmeni ghlossa (The forbbiden language), Kratiki katastoli ton slavikon dhialekton stin elliniki Makedhonia (State obstructions to the Slavic dialect in Greek Macedonia), Athens.

—— 2003, *Counting the „Other": Official Census and Classified Statistics in Greece (1830–2001)* in „JGKS" no 5.

Koufis, Pavlos 1994, Laoghrafika. Alona–Armensko Florinas (Folklor of Alona–Armensko Florina), Athina.

—— 1996, Laoghrafika. Florinas–Kastorias (Folklor of Florina–Kastoria) , Athina.

Kousoulas, DG 1965, Revolution and defeat: the story of the Greek Communist Party, OUP, London.

Kowalski, J, Lemantowicz, W & Winczorek, P 1983, Teoria państwa i prawa (The theory of state and law), Warsaw.

Kramer, CE 1999, Macedonian: A course for beginning and intermediate students, Univ. of Wisconsin Press, <http://www.wisc.edu/wisconsinpress>

Kruševski manifest (The Kruševo manifesto), 1983, INI, Skopje.

Kurlansky, M 1999, The Basque history of the world, Walter & Co., New York.

Kurtuluş, Ö 2006, Elementary Turkish: A Complete Course for Beginners, Santa Monica–Istanbul.

Lange-Akhund, N 1998, 'The Macedonian question 1893–1908: from Western sources', East European Monographs, Boulder, distrib. by Columbia Univ. Press. New York.

Lehr–Spławiński, T (red.) 1949, 'Teksty południowo-słowiańskie (ze słownikiem)' (South Slavonic texts (with dictionary)), (Cz. I) (Part I), Chrestomatia słowiańska (Slavic chrestomatia), Wydawnictwo Studium Słowiańskiego Uniwersytet Jagielloński, Skład Główny Księgarni "Ossolineum", Kraków.

——, Kuraszkiewicz, W & Sławski, F 1954, Przegląd i charakterystyka języków słowiańskich (Review and the characteristcs of the Slavic languages), Warsaw.

Lenin, W I 1952, O prawie narodów do samookreślenia (On the right to self-determination of nations)), Warszawa.

Lewis, B 1972, Narodziny nowoczesnej Turcji (The emergence of modern Turkey), Warszawa.

Lithoxoou, D 1998, Ellinikos antimakedhonikos aghonas, A': Apo to Illinten sti Zagkoritsani (1903–1905) Athens, 2007, (The Greek anti–Macedonian struggle 1: From St. Elias' to Zagorichani (1903–1905)), Az-Buki, Skopje.

Litoksou, D 2005, Izmešana nacija ili za Grcite i raznebitenite drugojazičnici, Az-Buki, Skopje.

Ljorovski-Vamvakovski, D 2017, Germanos Karavangelis. Grčkata propaganda vo Kosturska eparhija (1900-1903) (Germanos Karavangelis. The Greek propaganda in the Kostur eparchy (1900-1903).

Ludy i języki świata, (ed. Damm K and Mikusińska A) 2000, Wydawnictwo Naukowe PWN, Warszawa.

Lunt, H 1965, The grammar of the Macedonian standard literary language, Skopje.

Macedonia and its relations with Greece, 1993, Skopje.

The Macedonian–Greek conflict: the age long conflict between the Greeks and the Macedonians, <http://www.historyofmacedonia.org/MacedonianGreek Conflict/conflict.html>

Macedonian heritage, < http://www.macedonian-heritage.gr>

'Macedonian language', Wikipedia, <http://en.wikipedia.org/wiki/Macedonian_language>

'Macedonian question', Wikipedia, <http://en.wikipedia.org/wiki/Macedonian_Question>

The Macedonian question in foreign relations, <http://www.historyofmacedonia.org/PartitionedMacedonia/Macedonian Question.html>,

Macedonians, < http://www.greekhelsinki.gr/bhr/english/articles/the_macedonians.doc>

'Macedonians in Greece', Wikipedia, <http://en.wikipedia.org/wiki/Macedonians_(ethnic_group)_Greece>, [pobrano: listopad 2011]., < http://faq.macedonia.org/history/12.1.2.html>

Mackridge, P 2009, Language and national identity in Greece, 1766–1976, OUS.

MacMillan, M 2002, Paris 1919, Random House, New York.

Majewicz, A 1989, Języki świata i ich klasyfikacja (Languages of the world and their classification), Państwowe Wydawnictwo Naukowe, Warszawa.

Małecki, M 1933 and 1936, Dwie gwary macedońskie (Sucha i Wysoka w Soluńskiem) (Two Macedonian dialects of Suho (Soho) and Visoka (Ossa) in the Salonika prefecture), Cz. I: Teksty (Texts), Cz. II: Słownik (Dictionary), Kraków.

Mango, A 2002, Ataturk, John Murray (Publishers) Ltd, London

Mangov, K 1995, Za makedonskite čovečki prava (On the Macedonian human rights), MRT – Makedonsko Radio, Skopje.

Martinova-Bučkova, F 1998, I nie sme deca na majkata zemja (We also are children of the Mother Earth), Skopje.

Matelski, D 2007, Tożsamość narodowa i procesy integracyjne Serbołużyczan w Rzeszy Niemieckiej (od średniowiecza do współczesności)(National identity and the integration processes of the Sorbs in the German Reich (from Middle Ages till modernity), in: Integracja i tożsmość narodowa w Europie Środkowo-Wschodniej na przestrzeni dziejów (Integration and national identity in Central and Eastern Europe throughout the history), Wyd. Neriton, Instytut PAN, Warszawa.

Meghali Gheniki Enkiklopedia Hydria, 1989, Athens.

'Metaxas Ioannis', Wikipedia, <http://en.wikipedia.org/wiki/Ioannis_Metaxas>

Michailidis, I 1996, 'Minority rights and educational problems in Greek interwar Macedonia: the case of the primer "Abecedar"', Journal of Modern Greek Studies, 14/2, ps.329–343, <www.macedonian-heritage.gr/downloads/library/Michai01.pdf>

Mihailov, M 2000, Prašanjeto na obedinuvanjeto na Makedonija vo Vtorata svetska vojna (The question of unification of Macedonia during the Second World War), Skopje.

Miller, A F 1983, Turcija. Aktual'nyje probliemy novoi i novieišiei istorii, Izdatiel'stvo Nauka, Moskva.

Misirkov, PK 1974, On the Macedonian matters, Macedonian Heritage Collection, Macedonian Review, Skopje, <HTTP://www.macedonia.org>, and <http://www.misirkov.org>

——1991, Odbrani stranici (Selected pages), Skopje.

Moch, GIJ 1935, Rewolucja w Hiszpanji (Revolution in Spain), Publ. Co. M. Fruchtmann, Warszawa.

Modern relations between Macedonia and Greece, <http://www.makedonika.org/html/modern_mk_gr_relations.htm>

Mojsov, L 1954, Okolu prašanjeto na makedonskoto nacionalno malcinstvo vo Grcija (Around the question of the Macedonian national minority in Greece), Skopje.

Muszyński, L 1984, Wstęp do filologii słowiańskiej (Introduction to Slavonic philology), Warszawa.

Nakovski, P 1987, Makedonskite deca vo Polska (1948–1978) (Macedonian children in Poland (1948–1978)), Skopje.

Nakratzas, G 1999, The close racial kinship between the Greeks, Bulgarians and the Turks, Batavia Press, Thessaloniki, (Macedonian transl. 2006, Tesnoto plemensko srodstvo na denešnite Grci, Bugari, i etničkite Makedonci, Bitola), <http://www.florina.org>, email g.nakratzas@wxs.nl

Narody mira istoriko–etnografičeskij spravočnik (Nations of the world historical–ethnographic guide), (ed. Bromlej, Ju V) 1988, Sovietskaja enciklopedija, Moskva.

New Encyclopaedia Britannica 1975, Micropaedia, vol. III.

Ortakovski, V 1998, Minorities in the Balkans/Malcinstvata na Balkanot, (English–Macedonian edition), Skopje.

——2000, Minorities in the Balkans, Transnational Publisher, Inc. Ardsley, New York.

Osvoboditelnato dviženie v Makedonija i Odrinsko: spomeni i materiali (The liberated movement in Macedonia and the Odrin district: memoirs and materials) 1983, vol.1-2, Fototipno izdanie na Izdatelstvo Nauka i Izkustvo, Sofija.

Padewski, J 1967, Historia powszechna 1871–1918 (General history 1871–1918), Warszawa.

Palmer, SE Jr & King RR 1971, Yugoslav communism and the Macedonian question, Archon Books, Hamden.

Pandevski, MD 1978, Ilindenskoto vostanje vo Makedonija 1903 (The Ilinden Uprising in Macedonia 1903), Skopje.

'Pangalos Theodhoros', Wikipedia, http://en.wikipedia.org/wiki/Theodoros_Pangalos_(general)

Paszkiewicz, J 2004, Jugosławia w polityce Włoch w latach 1914–1941 (Jugoslavia in the policy of Italy in the years 1914–1941), Wyd. Poznańskie, Poznań.

——2012, Grecja a bezpieczeństwo narodowe na Bałkanach 1923–1936 (Greece and the national security in the Balkans 1923–1936), Instytut Historii UAM, Poznań.

Pejov, N 1968, Makedoncite i Grag'anska vojna vo Grcija (The Macedonians and the Civil War in Greece), Skopje.

——1993, Zagovor protiv Makedonija: avtorski prologi i izbor na statii so komentar (Conspiracy against Macedonia: author's prologues and selection of articles with comments) , Makedonsko Radio, Skopje.

Pentzopoulos, C 2002, The Balkan Exchange of minorities and its impact on Greece, C Hurst & Co Publishers Ltd.

Perry, DM 1992, Macedończycy, Bułgarzy czy slawofońscy Grecy? Problem świadomości narodowej (Macedonians, Bulgarians or Slavophone Greeks? The problem of national consciousness), Sprawy Międzynarodowe, no. 7–12, ps. 111–128, Warszawa.

'Phanariots', Wikipedia, <http://en.wikipedia.org/wiki/Phanariots>

Piotrowski, J1983, Spór o Palestynę, Warszawa 1983.

'Ponti (Pondi) or Pontic Greeks', Wikipedia, <http://en.wikipedia.org/wiki/Pontic_Greeks>

Poplazarov, R 1973, Grčkata politika sprema Makedonija vo vtorata polovina na XIX i početokot na XX vek (The Greek policy towards Macedonia in the second part of XIX and in the beginning of XX century), Skopje.

Popovski, T 1981, Makedonskoto nacionalno malcinstvo vo Bulgarija, Grcija i Albania (Macedonian national minority in Bulgaria, Greece and Albania), Skopje.

Popovski, JSA (n. d.), Makedonskoto prašanje na stranicite od „Rizospastis" megju dvete svetski vojni (Macedonian question on the pages of "Rizospastis" between two world's wars), Skopje.

Portraits of our past: the Sephardic communities of Greece and the Holocaust, <http://www.sephardicstudies.org/portraits.html>

'Pouliopoulos Pandelis', Wikipedia, <http://en.wikipedia.org/wiki/Pantelis_Pouliopoulos>

Poulton, H 2000, Who are the Macedonians?, 2nd edn, C. Hurt & Co., London.

Przewroty i zamachy stanu: Europa 1918–1939 (Revolutions and coups: Europe 1918–1939), 1981,Warszawa.

Radin, AM 1993, IMRO and the Macedonian question, Kultura, Skopje.

'Rainbow political party of ethnic Macedonians in Greece', Wikipedia, <http://en.wikipedia.org/wiki/Rainbow_(political_party)>, or <http://www.florina.org>

Raychman J 1962, Dni świetności i klęski Turcji (The days of glory and defeat of Turkey), Warszawa.

——1973, Dzieje Turcji (History of Turkey), Ossolineum, Wrocław.

The rising sun in the Balkans: the people of Macedonia 1995, International Affairs Agency, Research Center, Turkey, Politecon Publications, Sydney.

Ristovski, B 1983, Makedonskata nacija (The Macedonian nation), Skopje.

Romsics, I 1999, Hungary in the Twentieth century, Corvina/Osiris, Budapest.

Rossos, A 2008, Macedonia and the Macedonians. A history, Hoover Institution Press, Stanford University.

——Rozmówki polsko–macedońskie (Polish–Macedonian phrase book), 2003, Kram, Warsaw, <http://www.wydawnictwokram.pl>

Ryszka, F 1985, Państwo stanu wyjątkowego (The country of the extraordinary state), Wrocław.

Serafinoff, M 1995, The 19th century Macedonian awakening, Univ. Press of America.

Schapiro, J S 1929, Modern and contemporary European history (1815 – 1928), The Riberside Press, Cambridge, Massachusetts.

Shashko, P 1991. 'The emergence of the Macedonian nation: images and interpretations in American and British reference works 1945–1991', Michigan Slavic Materials, vol. 37, Michigan Slavic Publ., Ann Arbor.

Shea, J 1997, Macedonia and Greece: the struggle to define a new Balkan nation, McFarland & Co., Inc., Publishers, Jefferson, North Carolina and London, <http://www.historyofmacedonia.org/MacedonianGreekConflict/shea.html>

Sierpowski, S 1989, Źródła do historii powszechnej okresu międzywojennego. Tom pierwszy: 1917 –1926 (Historical documents to general history of the interwar period. Volume one: 1917 –1926), UAM, Poznań.

——1973, Faszyzm we Włoszech 1919–1926 (Fascism in Italy 1919–1926), Wrocław.

——1998, Między wojnami 1919 – 1939, Część 1: lata 1919 – 1929 (Between wars1919 – 1939, Part 1: years 1919 – 1929) , Wyd. Kurpisz, Poznań.

Simovski, TH 1997, Atlas of the inhabited places of Aegean Macedonia, (Macedonian–English edn), Skopje,

<http://www.historyofmacedonia.org/MacedonianGreekConflict/Summary.html>

Šklifov, B 1973, Kosturskijat govor. Prinos kym proučvaneto na jugozapadnite bylgarski govori (The Kostur dialect. Contribution to the study of the south-western Bulgarian [sic] dialects), Izdatelstvo na Bylgarskata Akademija na Naukite, Sofija.

Skowronek, J, Tanty, M & Wasilewski, T 1988, Historia Słowian południowych i zachodnich (The history of Southern and Western Slavs), Warszawa.

'Slavic language (Greece)', Wikipedia, <http://en.wikipedia.org/wiki/Slavic_language_(Greece)>, accessed May 2006

Sławski, F 1962, Zarys dialektologii południowosłowiańskiej z wyborem tekstów gwarowych (An outline of the South Slavonic dialectology with a selection of dialectical texts), Warszawa.

Smith, M L 2005, The Ionian vision. Greece in Asia minor 1919-1922, C.Hurst & Co., London.

Stavrianos, LS 2000, The Balkans since 1453, Hurt & Co., London.

Stawowy-Kawka, I 1993, Macedonia w polityce państw bałkańskich XX wieku (Macedonia in the policies of the Balkan states in the XX century), Kraków.

——1993 'Stosunki między Komunistyczną Partią Jugosławii i Grecji w latach 1943–1944' ('Relations between the Communist Party of Yugoslavia and Greece in the years 1943–1944'), Balcanica Posnaniensia, VI, ps. 201–211, UAM, Poznań.

——1998, Ludność Macedonii–zmiana struktury narodowościowej w XX wieku (The population of Macedonia: changes in the national structure during XX century), Dzieje Najnowsze, no. 2, ps.27–41, Warszawa.

——2000, Historia Macedonii (History of Macedonia), Ossolineum, Wrocław.

Stefanowicz, J 1977, Bunt mniejszości. Współczesne separatyzmy narodowe (Minority rebellion. Modern national separatisms), Warszawa.

Stefou, C 2003, The Macedonian struggle for independence. Celebrating the 100th Anniversary of the 1903 Ilinden Uprising, Toronto.

——2005, History of the Macedonian people from ancient times to the present, Risto Stefov Publ., Toronto. <http://www.oshchima.com>

Steriov, T 1995, Grčki jazik (so razgovornik) (Eliniki ghlossa (me sinomilies) Greek language (with a phrase book)), PIP "Dobruševski", Bitola. [This is a very good self-study manual for Macedonians wanting to learn Greek as well as Greek-speakers with basic knowledge of Macedonian will benefit from this manual greatly despite the fact that all texts Greek and Macedonian are pararel. So texts and exercises are translated line by line which accelarates language learning very much. Very practical manual].

Stępnik, K 2011, Wojny bałkańskie lat 1912–1913 w prasie polskiej. Korespondencje wojenne i komentarze polityczne (The Balkan wars in the years 1912–1913 in the Polish press.The war correspondence and political commentaries), Wydawnictwo UMCS, Lublin.

Stojanov, P 1969, Makedonija vo vremeto na Balkanskite i Prvata svetska vojna 1912–1918 (Macedonia during the Balkan Wars and WWI 1912–1918), Skopje.

——1979, Makedonija vo politikata na golemite sili vo vremeto na Balkanskite vojni 1912–1918 (Macedonia in the policy of the super powers during the Balkan Wars 1912–1918), Skopje.

Şükrü, I H (September 2002), Jewish socialism in Ottoman Salonica, Southeast European and Black Sea Studies 2 (3): s.115–146.

Szulc, W 1980, Przemiany gospodarcze i społeczne w Jugosławii w okresie międzywojennym 1918–1941 (Economical and social changes in Yugoslavia in the interwar period of 1918–1941), UAM, Poznań.

Tanty, M 1968, Konflikty bałkańskie w latach 1878–1918 (The Balkan conflicts in the years of 1878–1918), Warszawa.

——1982, Bosfor i Dardanele w polityce mocarstw (Bosphorus and the Dardanelles in the Super Powers policy), Warszawa.

——2003, Bałkany w XX wieku: dzieje polityczne (The Balkans of the XX century: political history), Warszawa.

Taškovski, D 1967, Rag'anjeto na makedonskata nacija (The emergence of the Macedonian nation), Skopje.

Tchavdar, M (undated), Aegean Macedonians: identity politics, political activism, refugee memories, Nexus Reasearch Project, EHEES, Paris.

The foundation of the Modern Greek state. Major treaties and conventions (1830–1947) (red. Photini Constantopoulou) 1999, Ministry of Foreign Affairs of Greece, Kastaniotis Editions, Athens.

The succession laws of the Greek monarchy, http://www.heraldica.org/topics/royalty/greece.htm#Convention-1832|

The Treaty of Bucharest 10 August 1913, <http://www.historyofmacedonia.org/PartitionedMacedonia/Bucharest.html>

Todorovski, G 1984, Reformite na Golemite evropski sili vo Makedonija 1829–1909 (The reforms of the European Super Powers in Macedonia 1829–1909), vol. 1–3, Skopje.

Tokarczyk, R 1984, Współczesne doktryny polityczne (Modern political doctrines), Lublin.

Topolińska, Z 1995, Zarys gramatyki języka macedońskiego (An outline of the grammar of the Macedonian language), Jagiellonian Univ., Institute of Slavic Philology, Kraków.

Tošev, K & Stefanija, D 1965, A textbook of the Macedonian language, Skopje.

The Treaty of Bucharest 10 August 1913, <http://www.historyofmacedonia.org/PartitionedMacedonia/Bucharest.html>

'Treaty of Lausanne', Wikipedia, <http://en.wikipedia.org/wiki/Treaty_of_Lausanne>

Treaty of Peace with Turkey Signed at Lausanne, July 24, 1923, <http://www.lib.bye.edu/~rdh/wwi/1918p/lausanne.html>, 'Treaty of Sèvres', Wikipedia, <http://en.wikipedia.org/wiki/Treaty_of_S%C3%A8vres>

Triadafilopoulos, T 17-20 .09.1998, The 1923 Greek-Turkish exchange of population and the reformulation of Greek national identity, speech prepared at the conference entitled Exchange of Populations Between Greece and Turkey: An Assessment of the Consequences of the Treaty of Lausanne which took place at Oksford University.

Trockizm, <http://pl.wikipedia.org/wiki/Trockizm>

Tsoucalas, C 1969, The Greek Tragedy, Penguin Books.

'Turkish War of Independence', Wikipedia, <http://en.wikipedia.org/wiki/Turkish_War_of_Independence>

Vasilevska, C & Cvetkova MSA, (undated) Otvori i razgovaraj makedonski–angliski (Open and talk Macedonian–English), Institut za Turizam pri Fakultetot za Turizam i Ugostitelstvo, Ohrid

Vlahov, D 1950, Makedonija: momenti od istorijata na makedonskiot narod (Macedonia: moments of the history of the Macedonian nation), Skopje.

VMRO Obedineta 1991, Dokumenti i materiali (VMRO United, Documents and materials), book 1, Skopje.

——1992, Dokumenti i materiali, (VMRO United, Documents and materials), book 2, Skopje.

Volkan V. D, 2007 On Kemal Ataturk's psychoanalytic biography, in: International Journal of Turkish Studies, Vol. 13, Nos.1&2, University of Wisconsin.

Voss C (n. d.), Minorities in Greece: historical issues and new perspectives. Tagungsakten der von der Fritz Thyssen-Stiftung finanzierten Tagung. FU Berlin, 30.1.-1.2.2003. Sevasti Trubeta, Christian Voss, (=Jahrbücher für Geschichte und Kultur Südosteuropas 5), 219 S.

——2003, 'Macedonian linguistic and ethnic identity in Western Aegean Macedonia', Die Welt der Slaven, 48, ps. 53–68

——2003, 'The situation of the Slavic–speaking minority in Greek Macedonia: ethnic revival, cross–border cohesion, or language death?', In: Minorities in Greece: Historical Issues and New Perspectives, p. Trubeta, Chr. Voss =Jahrbücher für Geschichte und Kultur Südosteuropas, 5, ps. 173–187.

——2004, 'Language use and language attitudes of a phantom minority: The Slavic–speakers in Greek Macedonia', in: Skrivene manjine na Balkanu, B. Sikimić. Belgrade, ps. 51–65.

——2006, 'Toward the peculiarities of language shift in northern Greece', In: Marginal linguistic identities: Studies in Slavic contact and borderland varieties, D Stern, C Voss, Wiesbaden, (=Eurolinguistische Arbeiten, 2):,ps. 87–101.

Votsis, PG 1998, Makentontseto (The little Macedonian boy), Ekdhosis Plethron, Athens, (Macedonian transl. 1999, Makedončeto, Skopje).

Vukmanović-Tempo, S 1982, Borba za Balkanot (Struggle for the Balkans), Skopje.

Walkiewicz, W 1998, Stosunki bułgarsko–jugosłowiańskie 1941–1948: uwarunkowania i implikacje (Bulgarian–Yugoslav relations 1941–1948: conditions and implications), SGGW–AR, Warszawa.

Wasilewski, T 1988, Historia Bułgarii (History of Bulgaria), Ossolineum, Wrocław.

Watson, C 1994, Ethnic conflict and the League of Nations: the case of Transylvania, 1918–1940, Hungarian Studies 9/1-2, Akademiai Kiado, Budapest.

——2003, Modern Basque history: eighteenth century to the present, Univ. of Nevada Press.

Wereszycki, H 1986, Historia Austrii (History of Austria), Ossolineum, Wrocław.

Wituch, T 1980, Tureckie przemiany: dzieje Turcji 1878–1923 (The Turkish changes: the history of Turkey 1878–1923), Warszawa.

Wojciechowski, S 2002, Integracja i desintegracja Jugosławii na przełomie XX i XXI wieku (Integration and desintegration of Yugoslavia at the turn of XX and XXI century), Institute of Political Science and Journalism, Adam Mickiewicz Univ. in Poznań, Poland. Tel. +4861 829 21 06

Wojecki, M 1989, Uchodźcy polityczni z Grecji w Polsce 1948–1975 (Political refugees from Greece in Poland 1948–1978), Jelenia Góra.

Woodhouse, C M 1998, Modern Greece. A short history.Faber and Faber, London.

World Communism: a handbook 1918–1965, (ed. Sworakowski, WS) 1973, Hoover Institution Press, Stanford.

Wyder, G 1998, Kwestia łużycka w świetle literatury historycznej okresu miedzywojennego (próba wstępnej analizy) (The Sorbian question in the light of the historical literature of the interwar period (an attempt of initial analysis)) , Wyższa Szkoła Pedagogiczna im. T. Kotarbińskiego, Zielona Gora.

'Young Turks', Wikipedia, <http://en.wikipedia.org/wiki/Young_Turks>

Zieliński, B (ed.) 2002, Wokół Macedonii: siła kultury–kultura siły (On Macedonia: power of culture–culture of power), Adam Mickiewicz Univ. Press, Poznań, <http://main.amu.edu.pl/~press>, [This book was published separately in Polish and English editions]

Zlatna Kniga: 100 godini VMRO (Golden Book: 100 years of VMRO) 1993, Skopje.

Znamierowska–Rakk, E 1991, Sprawa Tracji Zachodniej w polityce bułgarskiej (1919–1947) (The question of Western Thrace in the Bulgarian policy (1919–1947)), Instytut Historii PAN, Warszawa.

Zografski, D 1990, Za makedonskoto prašanje (On the Macedonian question), Skopje.

Zurcher, E J 2013, Turcja. Od sułtanatu do współczesności (Turkey. A modern history), Wyd. Uniwersytetu Jagiellońskiego.

INDEX

MAPS

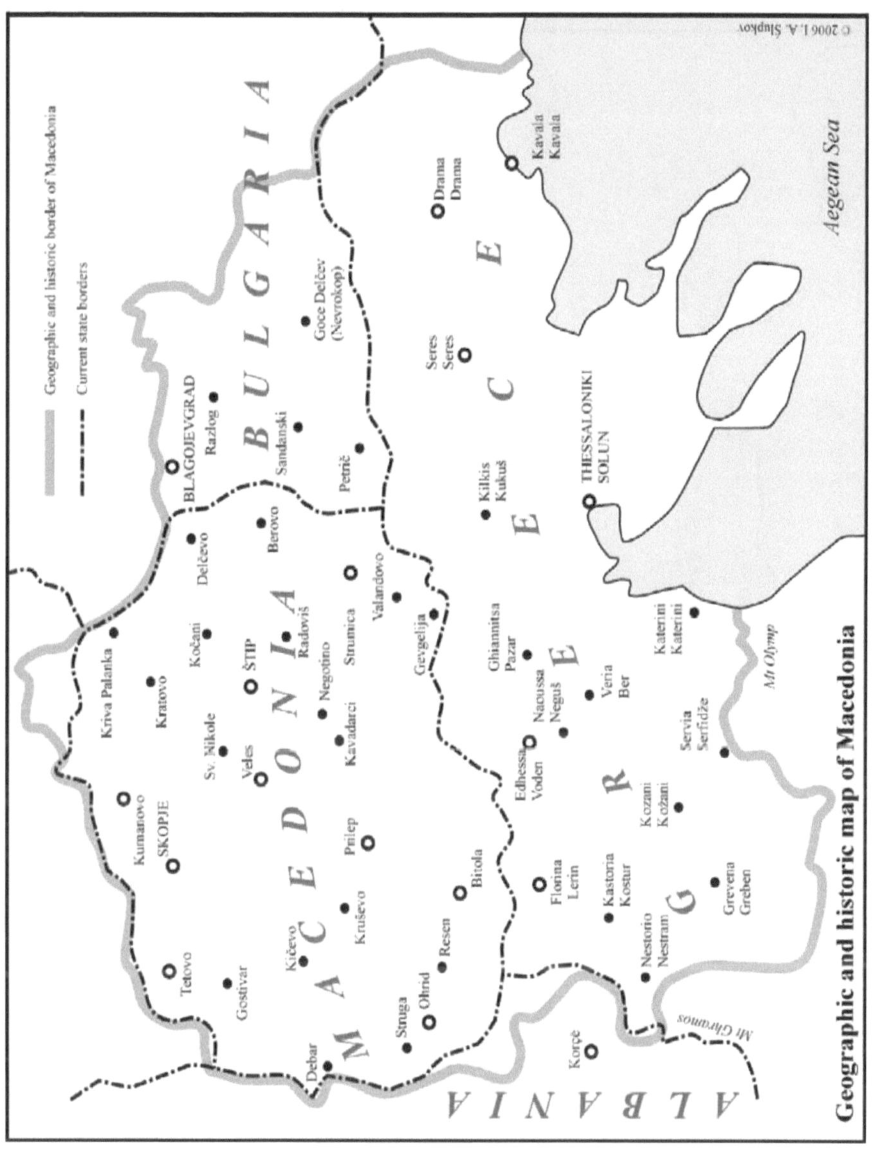

Geographic and historic map of Macedonia

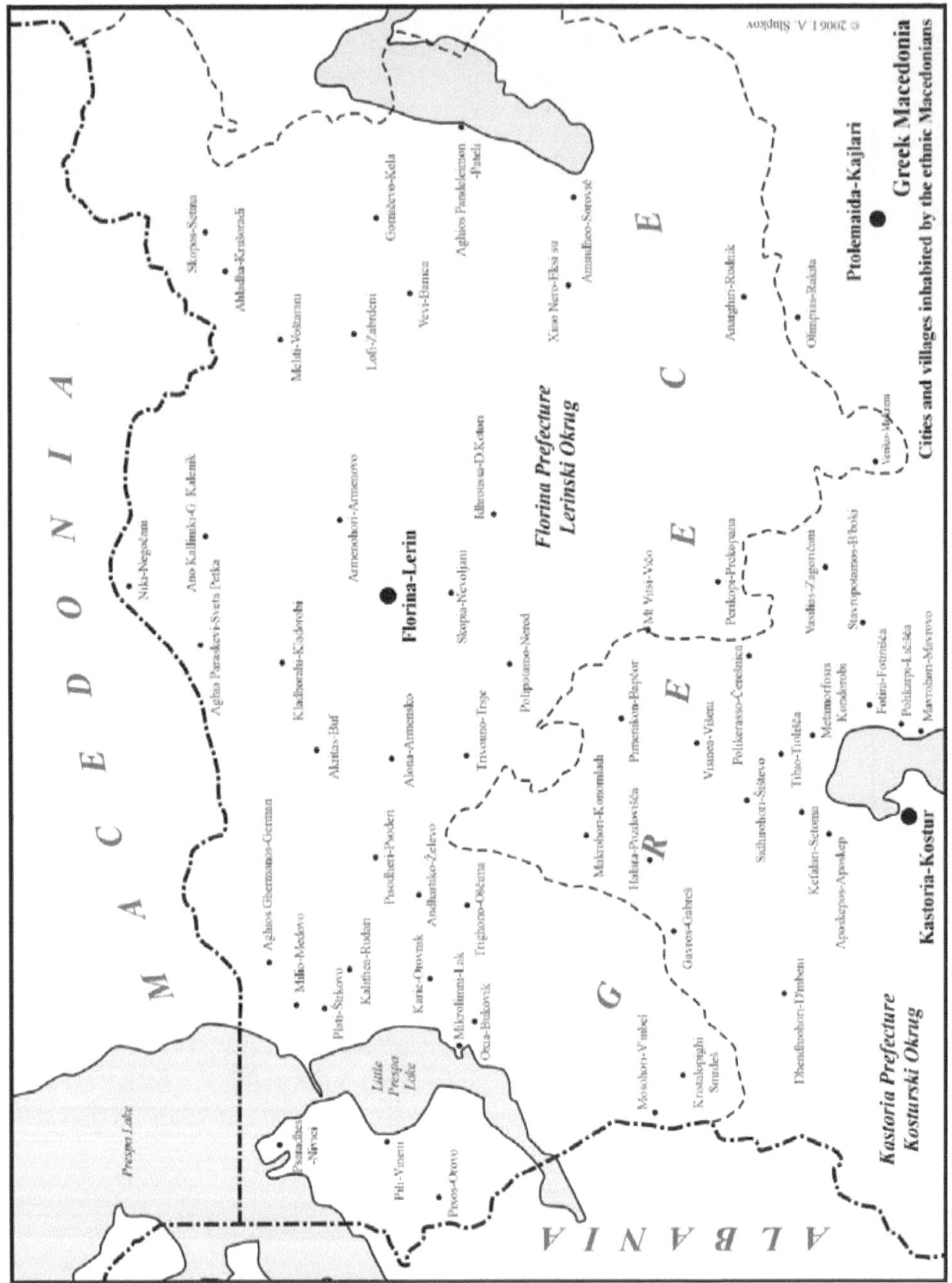
Greek Macedonia
Cities and villages inhabited by the ethnic Macedonians
M A C E D O N I A
G R E E C E
A L B A N I A
Florina Prefecture
Lerinski Okrug
Kastoria Prefecture
Kosturski Okrug
Florina-Lerin
Kastoria-Kostur
Ptolemaida-Kajlari
Little Prespa Lake
Prespa Lake

About the author

Ireneusz Adam Ślupkov was born on February 19, 1965 in Szczecin, Poland. He garduaded from the History Institute of Szczecin University. He started his master thesis under the direction of early died Professor Włodzimierz Pająkowski and continued further under the direction of Dr. Antoni Giza. His interests concerned the national minorities in Europe and the Macedono-Greek relations in the XX century. In 2000 he got a grant from Reno University, USA for learning the Basque language at the Basque Country University (Euskal Herriko Unibertsitatea) at Leioa, Spain which he started in January 2001 participating in the USAC program directed by Professor Félix Menchacatorre Egaña. During his studies he got acquainted with the situation and status of the Basque language in Spain (he was helped by Alan King, Begotxu Olaizola Elordi and Michael Morris). He also participated in classes in Basque history under the guidance of Professor Dr Cameron Watson (*Modern Basque history: eighteenth century to the present*).

A year later he stayed three months in Catalonia getting acquainted with the situation of the Catalan language and its status and with the national aspirations of Catalans. He participated in many seminars and meetings organized by Sorbs in Lausitz, Germany and got acquainted with the situation and status of the Upper and Lower Sorbian language in Germany.

Since 1991 he has maintained the contact with his master and mentor Professor Dr Stojan Kiselinovski the biggest authority on the CPG policy towards the Macedonian problem in Greece, ethnic changes in Macedonia and the Balkans in XX and XXI century and the lexical changes in the Macedonian language and its lexical and phonetic deformation under the influence of the Serbian language.

In 2006 he published a book *The Communist Party of Greece and the Macedonian national problem 1918-1940.* In 2011 he published altered and enlarged version of this book in Polish *Macedoński problem narodowy w Grecji w dokumentach Komunistycznej Partii Grecji 1918-1940.* On 27 June 2014 its first issue of his book appeared in the Czech Republic as *Makedonská národnostní otázka v Řecku v dokumentech Komunistické strany Řecka v letech 1918-1940.*

In 2018 he will publish the second edition of this book in Polish and second enlarged version in English and first edition of a new book in Polish *Sytuacja Macedończyków w Grecji i Basków w Hiszpanii i Francji.Studium porównawcze* (*Situation of Macedonians in Greece and Basques in Spain and France. A comparative study*) a synthetic depiction of an unsolved Macedonian problem in Greece and its comparison with the situation of Basques in Spain and France.

He participated in many European conferences regarding European national minorities (Basque Country, Greece, Lausitz (Germany)) and the human rights (OECD-Warsaw).

He commands fluently in three languages: Polish, English and Macedonian and understands in varying degree: Bulgarian, Spanish, Russian, Slovak, Serbian and Italian.

www.ingramcontent.com/pod-product-compliance
Ingram Content Group UK Ltd.
Pitfield, Milton Keynes, MK11 3LW, UK
UKHW041942190726
13854UKWH00004B/1753

9 780359 320172